Adoniram J. Rich

Historical Discourse

delivered on occasion of the one hundred and twenty-fifth anniversary of

the Congregational church, and the fiftieth anniversary of the Sunday

school, in Westminster, Mass., September 9, 1868

Adoniram J. Rich

Historical Discourse
delivered on occasion of the one hundred and twenty-fifth anniversary of the Congregational church, and the fiftieth anniversary of the Sunday school, in Westminster, Mass., September 9, 1868

ISBN/EAN: 9783337262242

Printed in Europe, USA, Canada, Australia, Japan

Cover: Foto ©ninafisch / pixelio.de

More available books at **www.hansebooks.com**

HISTORICAL DISCOURSE

DELIVERED ON OCCASION OF THE

One Hundred and Twenty-Fifth Anniversary

OF THE

CONGREGATIONAL CHURCH,

AND THE

Fiftieth Anniversary of the Sunday School,

IN

WESTMINSTER, MASS.,

September 9, 1868,

By A. JUDSON RICH,
(THE PASTOR.)

WITH APPENDIX.

SPRINGFIELD, MASS.:
SAMUEL BOWLES AND COMPANY, PRINTERS.
1869.

NOTE TO THE READER.

This Discourse, essentially the same as when delivered, has since that time undergone a careful and thorough revision. Every possible assistance has been summoned, through an extensive correspondence, and by a careful research of private, Church, and Town Records, and of State Historical Societies, that an accurate, an impartial, and a reliable history might be presented to the reader. A serious hindrance to the desired end, arose from the fact that the Records of the Church during the sixty-five first years of its existence, were accidentally lost many years ago; and could not, except in a measure, be restored by any and all other means. Persons noticing errors or deficiencies, will oblige by communicating the same to the

AUTHOR.

WESTMINSTER, *March* 1, 1869.

DISCOURSE.

THEN SAMUEL TOOK A STONE, AND SET IT BETWEEN MIZPEH AND SHEN, AND CALLED THE NAME OF IT EBEN-EZER, SAYING, "HITHERTO HATH THE LORD HELPED US."—*I. Sam. vii.* 12.

THE setting up of memorials in commemoration of victorious events, is a custom coeval with the history of man. The custom had its origin in a sense of gratitude; and in the case referred to in the text, of gratitude to Almighty God for a signal deliverance wrought by Him in behalf of the Israelites. In view of this victory Samuel erected a stone as an enduring and a grateful memorial to the glory of God, and for the encouragement of Israel. The reason for the name given,—Eben-ezer, "Stone of help,"—being, that hitherto the Lord had helped them. Notwithstanding the history of the past had not all been victory or success, yet in view of all God's mercies, and especially of the last deliverance, it seemed proper to memorialize the event, and thus to stir within the hearts of all Israel a sense of gratitude, and the constant recognition of the fact to succeeding generations, that God is the strength and portion of his people forever.

Prompted by such sentiments and by such a spirit, we have met here to-day to erect *our* "Stone of help," to set up a memorial that shall be a constant reminder to our children's children, that "Hitherto the Lord hath helped *us*," as a church. One hundred and twenty-five years have passed since our fathers founded the Congregational Church in Westminster. To commemorate that event are we met to-day in this house of God.

From widely separated parts of the country, from interests and callings differing according to tastes and circumstances, and the influences that have helped to shape and mould our conditions and our lives,—we have gathered around the loved and honored mother. I may not say aged mother, since, inspiring thought, the Church never grows old. Here have we gathered to pay that tribute of respect ever cherished in the bosom of a filial heart. And it seems fitting that we should together recount the more important incidents of her career, and thus foster the spirit of love and reverence, and strengthen the bond of mutual attachment.

And while it moves us to gratitude for the cherished past, may it not inspire us with fresh hope as a church, "to remember the days of old, and consider the years of many generations," in which we may see the hand of God, and gratefully acknowledge his goodness, and his abiding love.

HISTORY OF THE CHURCH.

But coming to the history of this church. Go back in your thoughts a century and a quarter. Imagine a dense wilderness, far away from village or town in the northern part of the State, among the hills, between the Wachusett and the Monadnock mountains, and not even a "bridle path" from Lancaster the nearest settlement, some sixteen miles distant; and two years before, with not even a marked road from that place to this; picture to yourself the woods resounding with the howl of the wolf, the shriek of the owl, the gobbling of the wild turkey, and the savage yell of the Indian, who had not ceased to hunt these forests or to catch fish in these ponds, the smoke of whose wigwams only told where savage foes were marking the white man for destruction; and at a time when only two or three clearings were begun, and they upon the highest hills of this region, and only four families, and they poor, and living in extemporized houses of logs or hewn timber, sixteen by twenty-two feet:—imagine that at such times, and under such circumstances, so dark and forbidding, a house of worship was built and dedicated to God; and the glad notes of the gospel sounded forth from the lips of the preacher, and the wild woods which covered these hill-tops rang out with the sound of prayer and praise to the great and good Spirit, the Almighty Father.

It was three years after the erection of the first church edifice, that a Church was organized. And at that time the settlement had been re-enforced by only two or three families. Thus it becomes apparent that the founders of this church were men of faith, and courage; a brave and hardy band, fearless of danger, true to Puritan principles, and loyal to Christ.

But the setting up of the worship of God in this dense wilderness, exposed to the savage cruelty of the sons of the forest, and remote from civilized man, was only in keeping with the spirit of New England's early ancestors.

The Puritans were somewhat bigoted and intolerant; but their love of soul-liberty, their stern, solid and transparent piety, their high-toned, devout Christian manhood, their kinship with truth, and their alliance by faith and prayer with the Almighty, fitted them to be the true pioneers of a nation, and the conservators of human rights, which lay at the foundation of a democratic government. They founded this government, the best under heaven; and the "Mayflower" and "Plymouth Rock" will be forever linked with the true ideal of nationality. And inheriting, as we have, from them such a boon in a pure religion and a Christian State, we can well afford to pardon their weaknesses, and to cover their sins in minor matters, and to let the mantle of charity and of a willing silence rest upon their memory forever.

The early settlers of this town and the founders of this church were directly from the noblest stock and the best blood of the Puritans. They were from Woburn, Watertown, Newton, Cambridge, Charlestown, Lancaster and other towns of early settlement. The history of this parish for more than seventy-five years was identical with the history of the town. Thus it may be pertinent to allude to the early history of the town, before its incorporation.

SETTLEMENT OF THE TOWN.

Narraganset No. 2, the name given to this tract of land, until its incorporation into a District in 1759, when it took the name of Westminster, from ancestral associations in the motherland—though it was not incorporated into a town till 1770—was so called from the fact that it was territory set apart by the General Court in 1728, for the remuneration of the descendants of the soldiers for the services of their fathers, fifty years before in the war with the Narraganset Indians, or King Phillip's war; a war lasting about one year, at the sad cost of six hundred lives and as many houses. In casting lots for the townships, it was agreed that the company which should draw No. 2, should assign 500 acres to His Excellency Governor Belcher, for his honored father's right. On casting lots, James Lowden for the company from Cambridge, &c., received No. 2. And the Governor built a mansion on the lot, and spent part of his time in his forest home.

At the first proprietors' meeting, December 28, 1733, they directed the Dividing Committee to fix upon a place for house-lots, His Excellency's farm, and "a proper place for a meeting-house." And they laid out land sufficient for a meeting-house, a training-field, and burying-ground. Then a lot for the first settled minister, a lot "for the ministry," and another for schools ; thus early recognizing the duty of worshiping God, of the support of the ordinances of the gospel, the cause of education, and of maintaining the principles of civil and religious liberty. The church, the school-house, the sword and the burying-ground—exponents and symbols of man's privileges, duties and destiny.

The place selected for the meeting-house, was on the "Hill," where the two first meeting-houses were erected, now known as "the Common." Lot No. 8, now Mr. John Minott's farm, was assigned to the first settled minister, and lot 95 to be the "ministerial lot."

Captain Fairbanks Moore from Lancaster, was the first who removed his family into the place, which he did in March, 1737, and only two years before the dedication of the first meeting-house, which according to Whitney's valuable History, published in 1793, was "a decent house ;" and five years previous to the organization of the church. The order was, first a dwelling-house, then a meeting-house, then a minister, then a church, then a school-house.

MINISTERS.

In reliable documents we find it recorded that "the settlers on the 4th day of August, 1742, made choice of Elisha Marsh, a graduate from Harvard College, for their minister." From January, 1738, as soon as two families were settled, up to 1742, the gospel was supported in town. The first money voted for the support of preaching was one hundred dollars, January, 1738, and another hundred the following December; and two hundred dollars, annually, from this time was appropriated for that purpose until a clergyman was settled in the township. The supply probably came from Harvard College, there having been no "13 Cornhill, Boston," as now. Mr. Marsh's settlement took place October 20, 1742, at which time he was publicly ordained to the gospel ministry, and the church was "embodied." His salary was fixed at one hundred and fifty dollars, in addition to the land to which he was entitled by the grant.

After the ordination of Mr. Marsh,—a little uncongregational,—the church proceeded to organize itself, and on the same day, chose Joseph Holden, and Joseph Miller, deacons, who served in their offices until death closed their faithful services, Mr. Miller holding his office fifty-two years.

REV. ELISHA MARSH.

From what we learn of Mr. Marsh, he was a man of considerable talent, but of much eccentricity of character, not comporting with what was then regarded as ministerial dignity. Soon after his settlement, an unhappy controversy arose between him and his people, which ended in his dismission in 1757. During a large part of this period, their relations were anything but happy. He seemed to regard himself and the church as two distinct parties, and one member of the church with himself, it is said, always made a majority. But the fault was not all on his side. He evidently had an unyielding people to contend with, and they had no patience with the exuberance of their young pastor, fresh from college, and given a little to wit and humor. They tried every means to get rid of him; and when they withheld his salary, he would sue the town. A threat to sue in 1755 induced the town to call a town meeting, when they "voted to give to Mr. Marsh all his back pay."

His conduct and sayings were laid before councils, which were at last induced to sunder the ties which bound him to the parish, and which were probably intended to be of a lifelong character, as was the custom in those days in the settlement of a minister.

Some of the charges preferred against Mr. Marsh were characteristic of the times. One of them was for "stumping one of his church members on the Sabbath to swop powder-horn strings with him." And he was said to have stepped down from the pulpit, and in the sanctuary engage his help for the next day to work on his farm. It was also thought that he was heretical. The following charges were preferred against him: "For saying that obedience is the condition of salvation;" and that "he would as soon worship the devil as worship such a being as requires more from his creatures than they are able to perform;" for saying that "if all that was required of a man was to believe, then the condition of salvation was easy and pleasant to fools." Not a bad theology, we are inclined to think, for the nineteenth century. Whether they failed to prove these "serious charges," or whether the association at Lancaster, before which they were brought, failed to see heresy in them, is uncertain. They did not dismiss him till ten years after his trial. The originality of his language, and the keen force of his logic, so wittily and boldly expressed showed that he was a person of no ordinary mind, but possessing, if not much devotion, yet a good deal of common sense, and of faith that was eminently practical. He was sometimes in lawsuits with the town, and at one time while pleading his own case before some referees, Mr. Heywood* being one of them, and noticing that he had become a little excited, checked him in his fervor; his reply was:—"*Its my zeal—I was always a zeal-ous preacher.*" No doubt he was naturally a little hot-headed, and perhaps a little rash in his conduct, but well meaning. His ready wit was manifested one morning on meeting the sheriff from a neighboring town, who, being on his way to sue the town, and as was the custom to serve the writ on some one of the citizens, served it on him, saying in a pleasant manner, as he handed him the writ: "The grace of God, Mr. Marsh." "Yes, by the hands of the Devil," was his quick retort.

After Mr. Marsh was dismissed from his pastorate which occurred in 1757, he remained some time in the township, filling several secular offices. He at length removed to Cheshire County, New Hampshire, and became Judge of the Court of Common Pleas. He died in Lancaster from injuries received from a fall from his horse while on his way to Boston, with a drove of fat cattle for market. His ashes still lie in that ancient and pleasant town; and his spirit, we trust, dwells in the realms of the blessed.

---

* Grandfather to the late William Heywood.

INTERREGNUM.

From the dismission of Mr. Marsh to the settlement of Mr. Rice, the church and society was in a broken and distracted condition. They had preaching the greater part of the time, but they were troubled with these terrible "divisions," the worst kind of which are ecclesiastical, and always, sad to say, are generally the hardest to heal, and the most disgraceful in their character, putting to the blush any secular litigations.

In 1760 a call was extended to Samuel Dix, but he declining, calls were subsequently extended to Messrs. Peter T. Smith, Samuel French, and John Wythe. Each in his turn declined the office. The feeble state of the society, and the unfortunate controversaries with Mr. Marsh, which continued after his dismission, undoubtedly had their influence in deferring the settlement of a pastor.

REV. ASAPH RICE.

At length, at a meeting held July 19, 1765, the society voted to concur with the church in extending an invitation to Mr. Asaph Rice, a Harvard graduate, to become their pastor. Mr. Rice accepted the call, and the 16th of October was fixed upon for the ordination, when he took upon himself the solemn duties of pastor. The sermon on the occasion was preached by Rev. Eli Forbes, of Brookfield, from I. Cor. ii. 2, and was entitled, "The Evangelical Preacher's Determination." The sermon was published, and it was an able and an interesting discourse.

Mr. Rice was settled for life, the common custom in those days, but a most vicious one, and often entailing lasting sorrow, and sometimes disgrace upon both pastor and people. But in this case it was otherwise, Mr. Rice was always greatly loved by his people.

Asaph Rice was son of Beriah Rice of Westborough, a descendant of Edmund Rice, an original emigrant. He was born May 9, 1733, and was graduated from Harvard College in 1752. He studied medicine, and practiced a short time in Brookfield. Early in his ministry, Mr. Rice lost his right hand, which must have been a serious loss to him. He fell from his horse while crossing Cambridge Bridge, and broke his wrist, and very singularly, a short time afterwards, while crossing the same bridge, and in the same way he broke it the second time. The injury proved so serious that it became necessary to amputate the hand; and ever afterwards he wrote his sermons with his left hand. A sermon written by his right hand from the words "what shall it profit" &c., was for a long time preserved by the family.

Before his settlement in Westminster, he spent some time in preaching to a tribe of Indians in *Rhode Island*, probably the Narraganset tribe, and not a tribe in the South, as commonly supposed. See Mrs. Jackson's letter in Appendix.

Mr. Rice married December 26th, 1765, Mary Morse of Royalston, Mass., daughter of Ebenezer Morse. She died the following year, in the 20th year of her age. He married for his second wife, Lucy Clough of Boston. She died, and he married for his third wife, Lucy Shattuck, widow of Benjamin Shattuck, physician of Templeton. She survived her last husband, about five years, and died at Templeton in 1821.

Mr. Rice's children were as follows: Persis, born November 1766; married Silas Beaman. Elizabeth C., born 1771 married Dr. Asa Miles. Thomas, born 1774; married Mary Eames of Boston. Asaph, died in infancy. Asaph, born February 17, 1777, entered Harvard College, 1798; married Abigail Sawyer of Boston. Mary, born January 1778; married Jacob Sawyer. Thankful, born 1780; married Farwell Jones. Mr. Rice had seven children, only one of whom is now living. His home is in the West, and he has reared a noble family of seven children, all of whom are living, and are members of the Church of Christ.

Mr. Rice continued his relations with the Society till his death, which occurred March 31, 1816, in the eighty-third year of his age, and the fifty-first of his ministry.

He was in his person a little above medium stature, well proportioned, rather spare, broad shouldered, with long face, large nose, and dark complexion. In the latter part of his life he wore a wig, after the manner of the times in which he lived. His voice was heavy and strong. He was a person of very great dignity, and gravity. And of course the children would not be attracted to him. From him as from most pastors of that day they would keep at a distance, and would not meet them if possible. This sobriety and gravity was thought to be necessary in a minister then. It never occurred to people that religion could be made attractive to young or old; or that it was anything but sinful to be happy and cheerful, or that religion was for beautifying and adorning every day life. And still, naturally very social, often spending his evenings out at some neighbors till a late hour, Mr. Rice had a power with the little ones, and would often take them upon his knee and teach them the catechism. He was a great peace-maker; and when politics ran high, would often resort to the giving up his right of suffrage, for the sake of peace. A doubtful policy, and a demand which no people ever ought to make of their minister. In becoming a minister, one does not cease to be a man, and a citizen.

Mr. Rice, as a preacher, was not fluent. His sermons were pretty long, sometimes tedious, especially to children. He preached from forty-five minutes to an hour, often more, and on special occasions *indefinitely*. He was somewhat Arminian in doctrine, but became, some thought, more orthodox towards the close of his life. He was naturally liberal, and catholic, no controversialist, but very practical for the times, endeavoring to build up Christian character in his people instead of educating them into sectarians by dwelling upon the distinctive features of orthodoxy; and thus he was very useful, was greatly beloved, and died lamented by all of every shade of religious belief and by the whole town. There were no revivals in his day; none were prayed for. Few joined the church under the age of 30 or 40, and often not till 60 or 70 years of age.

In Mr. Rice's day there was no fire in the church; and as soon as the services were over, people would rush out of doors and scatter off to the neighbors, and to taverns to warm up and take their lunch of brown bread and cheese, and now and then a mug of cider, and a few, occasionally, something a little stronger. It is possible that this "warming up," together with the desire to meet each other, the only time most would be able to do so for the week, had something to do with the "regularity of the people at church." We venture to say that people now are led to attend church from as sincere motives as they were in those elder days, and that there is as much religion now, on Sundays or any other days as there was then. Stern duty, long sermons and dry doctrines have been exchanged for sweet privilege, and a worshipful service. There is less cant, and a much more healthful piety, now, than a century ago.

At noon on Sundays, most of the women and children went to Mr. Rice's house. He had a very large old-fashioned fireplace in his kitchen, six or eight feet across, which would always be filled with wood glowing with tremendous heat during the intermission, and one or two other fires would be kept in other rooms, so that the women and children might all have an opportunity to get warm and eat their lunch, always and for all, the same, brown bread and cheese.

Mrs. Rice was a very kind-hearted, generous, benevolent old lady; and she would be around among them to see that children and all had a chance at the fire, so as to get well warmed before the bell called them to the afternoon services.

As Mr. Rice grew old and began to fail, his people were very kind to him; and his salary being very small, never more than five hundred dollars, almost everybody would carry in something. Some carried wood, some butter, or cheese, or potatoes or hay, or corn, or beef. So often would such gifts occur, and so little thought of that upon one occasion, a quarter of beef came to the front door, and Mr. Rice "ordered it around to the back door." And this giving was done cheerfully; and the small salary thus supplemented, became of greater value than an ample salary, and a lack of *expressed* sympathy and kindness. During the latter part of his ministry, he had but one service on the Sabbath, in cold weather, which gave general satisfaction to the people.

When he died, all felt that a good man had passed away. The people generally attended his funeral, and the Choir, of which Deacon B. F. Wood was a member, met to practice for the occasion. Mr. Cyrus Winship was the chorister. Mr. Cushing of Ashburnham, who was himself settled in that place half a century before he died, preached the funeral sermon. His remains were borne with slow and solemn tread to their last resting-place in the " old Cemetery ;" and the spot is marked by a slab reared by the hand of affection, but now too deeply overshadowed by a dense forest. Two of his wives were buried side by side with his own remains. The seeming neglect of these graves is somewhat relieved by the spontaneous and hearty interest felt to-day in commemorating their noble deeds, a more enduring monument than grassy mound or marble slab.

But it is a mistaken idea that time and money spent in beautifying the place where our dead lie, are wasted. Affection's hand can do no better service than tenderly to care for the sacred dust of loved ones. The tomb of Jesus was situated in the midst of a lovely garden, fragrant with sweet-scented flowers, and smiling with beauty and freshness. Utility may cry out against "this waste ;" but we may follow Christ in death as well as in life, and believe that service grateful to the Master, which chastens our own spirits and mellows our hearts.

REV. CYRUS MANN.

After Mr. Rice became enfeebled by age, a colleague was chosen to assist him in his labors. Garret G. Brown, and William Bascom, who settled in Fitchburg, and afterwards in Leominster, in turn received and refused to accept calls.

Mr. Cyrus Mann, fresh from college, came along without any recommendations, save his diploma, and received almost a unanimous call to settle,—there being but six negative votes in the whole town. His salary was fixed at six hundred dollars. He was ordained February 22, 1815. The sermon was preached by Rev. Mr. Rockwood of Westborough, afterwards of Swanzey, N. H., from Heb. xiii. 17: " For they watch for your souls, as they that must give account." The occasion was one of great interest in several respects. Few persons in town had ever witnessed an ordination, half a century having passed since the ordination of Mr. Rice. Considerable excitement was therefore raised among the people, and as was then customary great preparations were made to entertain all persons from all the surrounding towns who might be present.

The exercises were solemn and impressive. Several aged ministers were present from the neighboring towns, some of whom had ministered at the altar nearly half a century, whose whitened locks and venerable appearance added not a little to the solemnity and interest of the occasion.

Mr. Mann, we are told, was in his person much like father Rice; rather above medium height, with square shoulders, of dark complexion, black eyes, heavy eyebrows, spare, very sedate, rather stiff in his manners, dignified, solemn, reserved, apparently unsocial, measured in his tread, and toeing in as he walked, and with downcast eye. He rarely smiled, almost never indulged in a hearty laugh. He was a Puritan without any cant; rigid in his piety without asceticism; devout without being transcendental. But his austerity and reserve were the less observed the more intimately one became acquainted with him. In his pastoral visits or at any time he rarely conversed upon worldly matters, and perhaps erred in not acquainting himself enough with the common matters of every day life, and with human nature in general; by no means an isolated case among ministers. Children rather feared than loved him. He was old school in theology, a strong Calvinist, and in his zeal for Orthodoxy, sometimes exhibited, perhaps, a little of the sectarian spirit. He was naturally conservative, jealous of new measures, wanted his people never to attend any other church, but their own, and feared lest other beliefs should get foothold in town. Indeed he was unwilling that any other denomination should occupy ground, as he thought, consecrated to the Congregational faith and order. But he lived to see two other sects planted in town, and starting out from his society. Mr. Mann was thoroughly orthodox. He dwelt a good deal upon the terrors of the law, and the awful doom awaiting the finally impenitent. He was slow of speech, had a high, squeaking voice, but was solid, clear and logical; he was hardly what you could call a dry preacher. He was thoroughly in earnest, pungent, sincere. His sermons were well studied, and able. He had the name of being one of the best sermonizers in the County, and often preached on public occasions, such as ordinations, church dedications and the like. His great power was in the pulpit, notwithstanding that his voice was so against him. He preached with authority, as though heaven commissioned, and upon a great errand; and his messages always came with plainness, tenderness and love. His prayers were original, fervid, and fresh, always suited to the occasion, and hence never repetitious or tedious.

His preaching was to a large extent doctrinal. " He taught the people knowledge." He thoroughly indoctrinated them in the essential truths of the Bible, and thus laid the foundation for right Christian instruction, and for a symmetrical Christian character. If people were not orthodox, it was not for lack of orthodox preaching. But all could not enjoy this sort of preaching. To some it savored too much of denominationalism and sectarianism. It was for such, too distinctive, too dogmatic, too rigid and lacking in catholicity and the spirit of conciliation. And the result was a division. The liberal element withdrew. The lines of orthodoxy were straightly drawn by Mr. Mann, and the Universalist Society was organized, and soon became large and flourishing, under the guidance of several able ministers, and among them, Hon. Charles Hudson who officiated as pastor for many years. This was about the time when all throughout the State the lines between Orthodoxy and Unitarianism became distinct, and well defined, and they have remained so to this day; but with a better feeling all around ; with less bitterness, with more expressed charity, and in some cases, especially among the Methodists, with a tendency to fraternization with the liberals. And the time may come when people of different religious views can meet socially and civilly, if not religiously on the common platform of love if not of belief. The time has already come when Christians of all denominations emphasize points of agreement more, and lines of divergence less ; and when each is more willing to see in all others any truth which they may hold. And the millennial day will draw nigh in proportion to the degree in which we all imitate Christ in his life, and obey his teachings. And the nearer we are to Him, the centre, the nearer shall we be to each other. And it rejoices my heart to believe that in this community the spirit of mutual love and friendliness, predominates in the hearts of those who differ essentially in their religious faith. This is as it should be. It is as Christ would have it.

When Mr. Mann began his labors here, some thought the angel of mercy had come to lead them to the Savior, while others regarded him as the apple of discord to divide them in twain. His preaching was directed for the most part to the impenitent, to the neglect, as some thought, of instruction for the believer, his great anxiety for gathering in the wandering sheep causing him to forget that the flock should be fed as well as housed. Yet his people did not lack in doctrinal instruction.

He was of feeble health, and yet his great industry, perseverance, and method in work, enabled him to perform a vast amount of labor, and to succeed so admirably as he did in his ministry. He was thoroughly devoted to his work, and his heart yearned and burned for the salvation of men.

The following extract is taken from an obituary written by Dr. Cyrus Mann, and published in the Congregational Quarterly soon after his father's death :

"Rev. Cyrus Mann was born in Orford, N. H., April 3, 1785. He was graduated from Dartmouth College in 1806 ; taught an academy at Gilmanton, N. H., a high school in Troy, N. Y. ; and there he studied law, and was offered a lucrative place as partner with a prominent lawyer with whom he studied. In 1809, he was appointed tutor in Dartmouth College, holding the office for five years, where he wrote a treatise on trigonometry, which was used several years as a college text-book. He studied theology under the guidance of Prof. Shurtleff. He received a call to settle in Westminster, which he accepted, and was settled, remaining for twenty-six years and four months in successful and faithful service. During his stay here, there was almost a continuous revival of religion. *Four hundred and fifty-nine* persons were added to the church, one hundred and twenty during the first three years, and averaging eighteen per year for the entire period of his ministry. Precisely the same number of deaths occurred in the parish in the same period. He was dismissed from Westminster in June of 1841; preached at the Robinson Church in Plymouth, about three years, and at the Congregational Church in North Falmouth about four years. His last days were spent with his son, Dr. Cyrus Mann, then at Stoughton, where he died February 9, 1859.

At the ripe age of nearly seventy-four years, with confidence unabated in the doctrines which he had taught to others; and consoled most sweetly by the comfort of the cross to which he had so long pointed others, he passed away to his reward."

His aged and much respected Christian companion still survives; residing with her daughter, the wife of Rev. Mr. Norton of Fitzwilliam, N. H; formerly and for fourteen years pastor of the Congregational Church in Athol.

REV. STEPHEN S. SMITH.

Of the living pastors who have served at this altar, I may not be expected to speak at length.

Rev. S. S. Smith succeeded Mr. Mann in the ministry here, and was installed in the autumn of 1841, Rev. Dr. Smalley of Worcester preaching the sermon on the occasion.

Mr. Smith was educated as a printer, published a paper for some years; but having his attention called to the ministry, he fitted for college at Andover, but did not enter college on account of poor health.

He assisted Rev. Mr. Woodbury awhile in his pastoral work in Falmouth; received and declined a call to settle in Holden; accepted a call to settle in Quincy, where he labored two years under the Home Missionary Society; and gathered the Orthodox Church in that place; preached three years in a Presbyterian Church in New York; spent four years in the service of the American Sunday School Union; one year as assistant minister with Dr. Homer of Newton. Thence he removed to Westminster, where he spent eight years; and as many of the succeeding years in Warren as pastor of the Congregational Church; and since leaving that place, five years ago, he has been laboring as city missionary in Chicago, Ill., where he still continues to labor.

Mr. Smith came to this church under embarrassing circumstances. Towards the close of Mr. Mann's ministry a change in religious sentiment had taken place with quite a number of the leading members of the church. The doctrines of Calvin had to some extent been exchanged for those of Wesley, and the church was greatly divided on the doctrine of "Perfection." And unfortunately Mr. Smith came, according to his own words, "as the candidate of a party, expressly so understood;" though it was hoped and believed by his friends that he would harmonize all elements and heal all discords. Holding views in certain respects so diametrically opposed to the teachings of former pastors for a century, it was not strange that some friction and clashing should be the result. From this and other causes, Mr. Smith's ministry, though blessed with special religious interest, was on the whole rather stormy. His labors in Warren, and in Chicago have been, so far as I learn eminently successful. But sinking under the weight of years, he soon expects to lay by his armor and enter upon the reward of his labors.

REV. O. H. WHITE

Was ordained August 21, 1851, Rev. Dr. Pomeroy, whose daughter he married, preaching the sermon. Mr. White labored here for three years with great acceptance, and success. Under his ministry the congregation greatly enlarged through his popularity, and the church enjoyed an interesting revival, and an increase in membership at one communion of nearly forty persons. His excellent wife, respected and loved by this people, has since gone to her reward. Mr. White was dismissed from this pastorate August, 1854. He is now the pastor of the "West Church," in New Haven, Ct. A new and elegant stone church edifice has just been dedicated for the accommodation of the growing congregation of his charge.

REV. MARCUS AMES.

Rev. Marcus Ames succeeded Mr. White as pastor; being installed in May 1856. Mr. Ames was educated with reference to missionary labor, as physician in West Africa. But was hindered by circumstances beyond his control. And after laboring a few years in a church in Patterson, N. J., he came to Westminster, where he remained three years, laboring with great acceptance, and leaving with universal regret on the part of the people. He subsequently preached two or three years in North Chelsea; and in 1862 was elected Chaplain and Superintendent of the State Industrial School for girls, in Lancaster, where he still labors with great success.

About the time of his coming to Westminster, the church was divided on the American Board, and the Missionary Association. But sympathizing with both causes, and possessed of wonderful tact and great kindness of heart, and full of warm love to the Savior, he harmonized all difficulties, won all hearts, and did a noble work, whose influence reaches down to the present time. His theology was thoroughly evangelical, with a leaning towards Methodism. A good deal of religious interest was enjoyed during his pastorate; and at one communion some twenty, mostly young persons, came forward and took upon themselves the name of Christ. It was a season of peculiar interest, and long to be remembered by the pastor, the church and the young disciples.

REV. BROWN EMERSON.

Rev. Brown Emerson was installed June 7, 1859, and dismissed March, 1862. Mr. Emerson had been settled before and was quite well along in years. He was a man of good learning, sound and discriminating in matters of theology, and gave very good sermons. He was somewhat after the pattern of Mr. Mann in his religious views and general deportment. I have been unable to gather anything further of importance concerning Mr. Emerson or his labors; and I have failed to reach him by letter.

REV. MILAN H. HITCHCOCK,

Educated at Amherst College and Bangor Seminary, was installed December 18, 1862, subsequent to a six months' supply of the pulpit; and was dismissed, at his own request, February 20, 1867, after nearly five years of faithful and earnest labors. He had been sent, by the American Board as a missionary to Ceylon; but his wife's health failing, they returned to this country after a missionary life of about two years. He is now laboring with the Congregational Church in Winchendon, greatly to its prosperity, and to the satisfaction of the people. His theology was decidedly "old school." Concerning his labors here, it is not too much to say that a more faithful pastor, or a more thoroughly earnest Christian worker, never had the guidance of this flock. Large accessions were made to the church during his pastorate, some sixty, by profession and by letter.

REV. A. JUDSON RICH.

The present incumbent, was educated at Waterville College, the Theological Institution in Newton, and the Union Seminary, New York City, graduating from the latter in 1863. Originally a Baptist, he became convinced while in the Newton Seminary that the *form* of administration of the rite of Baptism was a matter of little importance, and that "close communion" was unscriptural, uncharitable, and in no sense in harmony with the spirit and genius of the gospel, and only calculated to divide the church, and to foster prejudice, and to impede the work of evangelizing and christianizing the world; and on leaving that Seminary, and entering the Seminary at New York, he united with Dr. J. P. Thompson's (Congregational) church of that city.

He was ordained and installed over the Village Church in Dorchester, soon after graduation, where he remained nearly four years. Resigning his pastorate, he at once received a call to take charge of the Union Church in East Bridgewater. About the same time he received a call to settle in Westminster, which he accepted; and was installed May 22, 1867, Rev. Dr. A. C. Thompson of Roxbury preaching the sermon.

It is quite remarkable that only three of the pastors of this church have been called away by death, and those the three first, Marsh, Rice, and Mann; and all the ex-pastors are holding important positions in the ministry. Mr. Marsh served as pastor thirteen years, Mr. Rice lived to preach his half century sermon, and Mr. Mann labored for twenty-six years; the average term of service of all being about fifteen years. It is a little singular that the names of seven of the pastors are monosyllables.

DEACONS.

This church has ever been blessed with a band of noble deacons. There have been twenty in all, twelve of whom have gone to their reward; four are absent, and four are with us; two of whom, Dea. Robert Peckham, eighty-three years of age, and Dea. Benjamin F. Wood, seventy-seven, resigned their offices some years ago. The present deacons are Frederick Whitney, temporarily absent, David W. Hill, and T. Dwight Wood, all lately chosen.

The following is a list of the deacons in the order in which they were chosen: Joseph Holden, Joseph Miller, Thomas Stearns, James Walker, Nathan Wood, Moses Thurston, Stephen Miles, David Whitney (who lived to be within a few months of a hundred years old), James White, John Murdock, Robert Peckham, Benjamin F. Wood, Edward Kendall, Sewall Barnes, Aaron Wood, N. H. Cutting, W. S. Bradbury, Frederick Whitney, D. W. Hill, T. Dwight Wood.

Dea. Holden was great grandfather to Dea. B. F. Wood, and Dea. Miller was great grandfather to Mr. Jonas Miller. Deacons Holden and Miller were both very worthy and influential men. Both had been members of the General Court. Dea. Miller performed a good deal of public business, filling the highest offices both in district and town for many years. His records were exceedingly accurate and trustworthy. In the trying days of the Revolution, he was called to act as selectman, treasurer, and representative, and was a member of the body which adopted the State Constitution.

Concerning Deacons Stearns, Walker, Nathan Wood, Thurston, and Miles, I have been able to learn but little, beyond the fact that they were good men and faithful in Christian duty. Dea. Nathan Wood was grandfather to the late Dea. Aaron Wood; Dea. Thurston was grandfather to Miss Mary Thurston; Dea. White was father to Mrs. Daniel Harrington. Deacons Walker and Miles have descendants in town, but not very near. Deacon Holden served the church in his office twenty-seven years, and Dea. Miller, fifty-two years, death alone cutting short their labors. The average term of service for all the past Deacons, is twenty-two years, each. It is a pleasing fact that all the living ex-pastors of this church testify in emphatic terms, to the strength and encouragement they have derived from the Deacons who have been their helpers; ever surrounding and sustaining them as the true Aarons and Hurs of the church.

Surely the prosperity of any church depends greatly upon the character and competency of her Deacons. It is very largely within their power to say whether the cause shall languish, and the pastor's courage fail, or whether both together shall rejoice in peace, prosperity and a loving harmony. How much they may do by way of free and loving intercourse with the pastor, and by sympathizing with him, and expressing to him their interest in the prosperity of the church, and in his personal success and happiness. Such a Deacon, to a very large extent, has this church of late been called to part with in the person of Aaron Wood, who died of a painful and protracted illness in the spring of 1867. His loss was a deep affliction to this people and to the community. Possessed of sound judgment, a warm heart, and a generous spirit, and deeply imbued with the spirit of his Master, he carried his religion into business life, in honesty, promptness, punctuality, faithfulness; and into the family and social life in love and affection, and especially in giving to his children the invaluable legacy of a religious culture; and he lived to see them all, seven in number, come into the fold of the church. His mantle we trust may fall upon his successors in office. His widow having since (now 1869) been called to part with two affectionate daughters, who sing in glory with their father, has the warmest sympathy of the whole church.

REVIVALS.

This church has shared largely in the revival spirit. It has had seven distinct and wide spread awakenings, and most of them were during Mr. Mann's ministry.

In the autumn of 1817, and the winter of 1818, a revival prevailed in town which was the first one ever enjoyed in Westminster. The religious excitement was great, and meetings were held for religious exercises in almost every part of the town; and in some cases they were continued every evening, and were well attended. In April, 1818, eighteen persons, the largest number which had ever before joined at one time, stood up to confess Christ. Among this band we find the names of Jonas Miller, Aaron Wood, Benjamin F. Wood, and Solomon Strong, afterwards Hon. and Judge Strong. Another revival occurred in 1825. Mr. Mann writes in his diary of July 4, "we have now had between forty and fifty hopeful conversions, since the revival commenced." He writes again in 1827, "we were blessed with special Divine influences, when about seventy became hopefully pious, the interest having been unbroken since 1825." There were many interesting cases of conversion. The most hardened, the quite young and the aged, students at the academy in later years, strangers happening in town, and absent persons returning by chance,—were swept into the current and experienced renewing grace.

In 1830 another powerful work of grace was enjoyed by the people. "Divine influences," writes Mr. Mann, "seemed to come directly from heaven, and to burst upon the people like an electric shock. Conviction was brief, and great joy was manifested, and intense love among converts existed. They were filled with overflowing delight in God their Savior, in one another, in older Christians, and in the truth which had made them free in Christ." Most of the conversions were from among the youth and middle aged, and some of them are present here to-day, as also others who began the new life in 1825 and 1827, as living witnesses to the mercy and grace of Christ.

As was usually the case in revivals, opposition was manifested in no ordinary degree; and the happiness of families was in some cases disturbed by this spirit. At evening meetings, harnesses were cut from horses, the doors of the vestry and school-houses, where the people met to pray, were blockaded; and it was proposed to raise a mob to put down the revival, some parents almost going frantic "lest their children should be drawn into the excitement and be ruined." And while some parents were sending for their absent children to return and come under the influence of God's spirit, others sent their children away to escape the "contagion." But God's grace was mightier than all human opposition, and the work went on to a glorious completion.

The revival entered the district schools, and children were led to rejoice in Christ. In District No. 7, taught that winter (1831) by Willard Allen, a devout young man, now residing in Holden, the interest was so great among the scholars, that sports at intermission, were given up for religious services, which in some cases occupied the hours of study. Some dozen of the scholars became hopefully pious, and to this day some of them are holding on in the way of holiness. Mr. Mann records in his diary about this time, that "protracted meetings were held in various towns; but that the most desirable seasons of awakening, were through the ordinary means of grace." It was very common then to hold "four days' meetings," and to give up business to a great extent and attend the meetings.

An interesting revival prevailed here in 1840, the year of Mr. Mann's twenty-fifth anniversary of settlement. In this sermon, dated February 16, 1840, he says: "How many thrilling reflections rush upon the mind at this moment! Blessed be the Lord God for all his goodness and faithfulness towards me. Now the Lord is appearing in his glory, again to build up Zion! Conversions occur almost every day." At the next communion season twenty-eight were added to the church, twenty-three of whom had been consecrated to the Lord in infancy by baptism, a marked illustration of the fulfillment of God's covenant promise, and an encouragement to parents, publicly to consecrate their offspring to the Lord.

This revival began among the Baptists, who held a series of meetings preceded by a day of fasting and prayer, January 1, 1840. The Spirit began to be poured out, and it was not long before the religious interest was general in town. Denominational lines seemed to have been obliterated, and the work went on. Meetings were held in the day time at the Baptist Church near the pond, and in the evening at the Congregational Church. A Mr. Remington was the Baptist minister, and being very earnest and somewhat sensational, he seemed to have great influence in arousing the people to religious thought and action. Mr. Mann, at first stood aloof from the meetings, and desired that his people should do the same. But they continued to go, and finally he followed them. Scores were converted, many of whom were members of the Sabbath Schools. About an equal number of converts joined the Baptists and the Congregationalists. Some of whom have died in the faith, and others live as ornaments to the church, and living witnesses for Christ.

But among the pure gold there was some dross. Error had its work to perform, and some became its subjects. "Millerism" began soon after to prevail and a number of these converts became its adherents. The revival, promising so much good, ended in sectarian prejudices, and a good deal of bitterness. Its termination saddened many hearts. All went on well till injudicious measures began to be taken for drawing denominational lines by the *immersion* of some converts. Then the work of grace stopped of a sudden, and not a single case of conversion took place afterwards; an experience realized in many revivals since, when sectarian propagandism takes the place of zeal for the saving of souls, and the promotion of godliness. O, when will the churches learn, that service for the Master is better than zeal for a sect, and that the building up of Christ's kingdom in the hearts of men is better than the strengthening of denominational walls! Many of the members of this church to-day are subjects of special religious awakenings. And our prayer to-day is, O Lord revive thy work in the midst of us; come and visit thy plantation, and remember Zion once more, and restore unto us the joy of thy salvation! Give us feeling and emotion, but above all give us grace to purify the heart and to correct the life, and to make us all better men and women, and more thoroughly penetrated with the Master's Spirit. Make us true and just and noble, full of love and good works, toward all men to-day and all our days right along and ever;—thus shall we be the true disciples of Christ, and heirs of the kingdom.

PRAYER-MEETINGS.

The history of prayer-meetings in this town is a matter of considerable interest, since it marks an era in the Christian churches of this region, and of the churches in general.

About the year 1806 a revival of religion was prevailing in Princeton, under the pastoral labors of Rev. Mr. Murdock. And some of the more zealous converts came over to the eastern part of this town, contiguous to Princeton, and set up religious meetings. They were held occasionally, and alternately at the houses of Daniel Foskett, John Estabrook, and Nathaniel Tottingham. These were the first religious conference meetings ever held in Westminster; and they were well attended for those days. Among the attendants, was Thomas Conant, then between eighty and ninety years of age, and who experienced religion under the preaching of George Whitfield. After a while Father Rice went down to see what was going on, since he was entirely ignorant of the character of such meetings. Upon witnessing one he highly approved, and applauded them. He prayed and talked, and among other good things, he said that "he thought we could thus strengthen and encourage each other on our pilgrimages."

These meetings thus inaugurated, have in some form been carried on in town from that day to this. About that time several conversions took place in the south-eastern part of the town, in the vicinity of these meetings; and among them were Daniel Foskett, and Mr. Tottingham, above mentioned, who were about forty years of age; they connected themselves with the Baptists;—and Mr. Joseph Wood, seventeen or eighteen years of age, who joined the Congregational Church; he afterwards became a minister. These early meetings raised considerable excitement in town; and the finger of scorn began to be pointed at those who attended them.

In the year 1810, Dr. Warren, whose father was a wealthy physician of Charlestown, came to this place and set up as a practicing physician. He was a very devoted christian, and was about the first man who took a decided stand on the side of orthodoxy in the centre of the town. He was instrumental in organizing the first prayer and conference-meeting in the village. He invited a number of young people to his lodgings one Thanksgiving evening, and held something like what is called a prayer-meeting.

Mr. Nathan Whitney, a venerable father in Israel, whose memory is fragrant in the hearts of many still living, opened his house soon after the commencement of these meetings, and welcomed them to his hospitable shelter and accommodations, and for a long time, in this and other ways he generously fostered this nursery of piety. And for two or three years the house of Dea. Peckham was gratuitously warmed and lighted for the purpose of holding the meetings of the church, evincing the deep interest which he took in the cause of religion and the welfare of this church. These meetings were afterwards held in the vestry in the Academy building, erected for the double purpose of prayer-meeting and school. They were there held for a long time until the present vestry was finished; since which time they have there been held, and deeply interesting scenes have there transpired.

The prayer-meeting is surely the life of the church; it is the altar where its sacred fires are kindled. It is also the thermometer, the spiritual gauge of piety in the church, and as Dr. Beecher once said, "the bellows which keeps the fire burning in the congregation, and together, with the preaching is of more value than the preaching itself." And when viewed in the light of privilege as well as of willing duty; and sustained with spontaneous and hearty interest, the prayer-meeting is to the church as the furnace to the engine, the battery to the electric wire; but not of so much value unless the piety generated there be lived out in daily life, and be seen and felt for good by contact with the world.

These meetings ought also to be characterized by more of cheerfulness and of the spirit of joy.

THE ACADEMY.

You will be interested in a brief account of the old Academy on the "Hill." As early as 1824, at a social prayer-meeting at Dea. Peckham's house, originated the idea of building a vestry. At least then and there it took definite shape. At the close of the meeting, Dea. Peckham proposed that a vestry be built. The proposition was favorably received, and it was decided by unanimous vote to undertake the enterprise, and $400 were subscribed on the spot, Dea. Peckham heading the paper with twenty dollars, and others following with more or less. A building committee was chosen of which Dea. Peckham was chairman. But on account of some business failures in town, the matter was delayed some three years. The building was not completed till 1829. Mr. Mann, the pastor, of course was the *leading* spirit in the enterprise, and more than any other one felt the need of such a building; and being deeply interested in the cause of education, he proposed that the two objects of a vestry and an academy might be combined. His proposition was acceded to, and the building was erected with that double purpose. And it was decided to have the upper story devoted to the purposes of a school, and the lower room for the meetings of the church.

Mr. Mann did a great deal for the academy, subscribing fifty dollars from his small salary to begin with, and his interest and efforts continued to be untiring. He obtained several hundred dollars from wealthy people from abroad to whom he made known his wants. He was deeply interested in the education of young men for the ministry; and through his influence many decided to enter that field, and pursued their preparatory studies at the academy, which had been the result of so much prayer and effort and self-denial. In Mr. Mann's diary of March 3, 1832, we find this entry: " I have been making a great effort to procure some apparatus for our academy, and have succeeded beyond my expectations. I have been to Boston and obtained an air pump, electric machine, chemical apparatus, microscope, magic lantern, etc., etc.; and I have secured several hundred dollars for the benefit of the Institution."

"So influential was this academy," says the Congregational Quarterly, "in promoting learning and religion in Worcester County, that if Mr. Mann had never done anything else, he would deserve the lasting gratitude of the people of Westminster, and the surrounding towns." At one time there were nearly two hundred students in the academy, many of whom were strangers, and a good many were fitting for Amherst and Dartmouth Colleges; and among the number of those who have studied at this academy, may be found the names of many leading men in all the professions, and in other walks of life. We may mention the names of Dr. J. P. Bancroft, physician of the Insane Hospital, N. H.; Representative Washburn of Greenfield, Hon. Whiting Griswold of the State Senate, and our own present Governor Bullock, whose "homesick days at the academy" in boyhood, have brightened into a clear and sturdy manhood. His untiring industry in study, his habits of church going, and his modest unassuming manner, were precursors of his rising greatness.

Other persons, mostly natives, who have attended the

academy, are: Isaac Cummings, M. D., physician in New York City; Joel Wyman, M. D.; Cyrus S. Mann, M. D.; Rev. Henry Cummings; Rev. Charles Kendall; Rev. William Heywood; Rev. Charles Whitney; Rev. Prof. Abel Wood of Meriden Academy, N. H.; Rev. Joseph Peckham; George Miles, M. D.; Rev. Mr. Harrington; Rev. Mr. Mandell; Rev. Mr. Clark of Natick; Rev. E. P. Baker; Clough Miles; Francis and Porter Heywood of Chicago; the late Samuel Whitney of Fitchburg; Edwin Upton; Dea. C. K. Wood; Franklin Wood; George Wood of California; Moses H. Wood; Abel Wood; and a multitude of notables too numerous to mention, among whom is Major General Nelson A. Miles, noted for being "the youngest General in the army."

The following persons have been teachers in the academy, viz.: Franklin Jones, the first teacher; W. C. Jackson, W. C. Clark, Josiah F. Clark, J. T. McCollum, J. H. Stearns, Nathan Allen, M. D., Robert Hitchcock, A. H. Merriam, J. Russell Gaut, Mr. Jefferds, Mr. Ingalls.

The academy building can be seen to-day on the old hill, *as it was*, only a little more bleached and dilapidated; thus perhaps, having greater interest for the stranger who long ago carved his name in the belfry, or who has since carved it upon the walls of fame. This may be our apology for its gray and ragged walls, and its tottering turret, soon, however to be thoroughly renovated, and to be the scene once more of busy study and of classic lore. And we trust that the fostering care of the town will invest it with the dignity of a "High School" in every sense, whose future shall add glory to its well-earned fame in the past.

THE CHOIR.*

This discourse would seem to lack an important feature, certainly its true ring, did it not contain a brief history of the Choir, connected with the church ; a choir known and noted for ts talent, unity and valuable services in Divine worship. And it is worthy of note that almost all the instruction given in music has been by teachers born and bred in town, from Abel Wood, Esq., to George F. Miller, Esq. 'Squire Wood kept the first singing-school ever conducted in town. He used to meet the scholars from house to house in different parts of the town. He taught six days in the week, three sessions a day and evening, three hours a session, and at the *exorbitant* price of $8.00 per month, and boarding himself! He did a great deal for music, sparing no pains in trying to keep the choir up to the proper standard, whose leader he was for many years. And after, through age, having taken his seat below, it often fell to him in absence of the leader to "pitch" the tunes from his pew. 'Squire Wood took a deep and hearty interest in all matters pertaining to the church, which he loved as he did his very life. He brought up a family of nine children all of whom became exemplary Christians, an honor to the church and a blessing to the world.

Ichabod Johnson and a Mr. Peters used to teach singing-school in early years. Luke Bigelow, Jr., played bass-viol and bassoon ; Jonas Miller succeeded Mr. Bigelow on the bass-viol, and played from 1816 to 1852, thirty-six consecutive years. Col. Asa Bigelow was a prominent singer ; John Bigelow was the noted violin player, and for forty

---
*See Appendix.

years a player and member of the Handel and Haydn Society, Boston, who together with Abraham and Alanson, his brothers, constituted the respectable and wealthy jewelry firm of Bigelow Brothers, Boston. Mary Merriam, now Mrs. Whitney of Boston, a noted concert singer, used to sing in this choir. George F. Miller, Esq., led the choir for ten years; he has led the choir in Royalston twenty years, and has taught three hundred and twenty-five singing-schools, and as our leader on this occasion, shows but few signs of age, and that in his profession he has assuredly kept up with the times. H. G. Whitney, Esq. was the efficient leader of this choir for some thirty years. Mr. Leander Hartwell is the present leader. It is only in justice to say that the female element in the choir has been very valuable.

Great account used to be made of singing on Thanksgiving and other public occasions. The choir would practice for six weeks before the day came round. At such times, all the singers and players on instruments came out, and you might have heard the bass-viol, violin, flute, hautboy, French horn, bassoon, and clarionet, in one commingled chorus. An offence surely it would have been to old Dr. Emmons, who ordered "that fiddle," the bass-viol, out of his church. But David would praise God on all kinds of instruments; and surely so far from being out of harmony with the true idea of worship, the instrument may assist the voice in expressing the secret and devout emotions of the heart. The service of song is a higher kind of prayer, addressing itself to the higher and better feelings of the heart, and to the nobler aspirations of the rational and devout mind. And we are touching the edge of a new day in which the service of song is to take a higher place in the public worship of God, and also in the schools, the home, the workshop and the field. Worship is the essential idea of sacred music, and should so be regarded.

THE SUNDAY-SCHOOL.

The era of Sunday-schools began in New England, about fifty years ago. The first one was started in Newburyport in Dr. Spring's church, in 1814 by a Miss Carter, who has ever since, and is still a teacher in a Sunday-school. The years 1816, 1817, and 1818 were years of prosperity in the establishment of Sunday-schools; and among the new schools started was the one whose semi-centennial we observe to-day. The cause of Sunday-schools received fresh encouragement that year through the valuable services of Rev. Mr. Mann, whose position will be understood by the following extract from a report of our Sunday-school made in 1838, by Dea. Bradbury:

"The formation of this school was the result of an inquiry of a committee appointed by the Association of Massachusetts, respecting the best instruction of the children and youth, of which committee our pastor (Rev. Mr. Mann) was chairman; and who proposed to some of the brethren of this church the plan of collecting the children during the intermission on the Sabbath for instruction. The suggestion was soon carried into effect, and formed the basis of the report which he afterwards made to the Association, which report was by them adopted. *From this sprang this Sabbath-school, and probably most others in the State!*"

Mr. Mann entered upon the work with great zeal, though he said we need not expect to see immediate results from it; but hoped we might raise up a generation who would see and feel the results hereafter. Mrs. Persis Sweetser,

Mrs. Mann's mother, who lived with them, was a very earnest and efficient Christian worker, and no doubt had a great deal to do about starting the school. Hours were doubtless spent at their home on the hill in devising the best means for carrying out the proposed enterprise. Indeed it was she who first invited the young misses of the congregation to her own house to spend the intermission at noon in Sunday-school exercises, the recitation of Bible verses, and of the catechism. About the same time, and perhaps on the same Sabbath, at the suggestion of Mr. Mann some time previous, three young men, B. F. Wood, Aaron Wood, and Jonas Miller, then about from twenty to twenty-seven years of age, brought together a few boys, only three or four, after much endeavor during the previous week, who with themselves proceeded to the old red school-house near the church, and spent the hour in prayer, and in instruction from the catechism, and in repeating texts of Scripture. Thus the nucleus of this Sunday-school was formed; and remarkable it is, had Dea. Aaron Wood lived a few months longer, these three young men would have continued the faithful and constant teachers in the school from that day to this, a period of *fifty consecutive years.* Dea. B. F. Wood and Jonas Miller, still remain as teachers in the school, and are here to-day to witness and share in the semi-centennial celebration of its organization, and with good prospects of serving many years more.

The school at first was very unpopular, especially among the males; and fifteen or twenty, from ten to fifteen years of age were all that could be collected for some time. Some would not send their children because they feared the teachers would expect to be paid for their services;

others because it was a new thing, and with them, of course fraught with evil; while others regarded it as too secular, frivolous, or as the introduction of unauthorized and perhaps troublesome and undevout "machinery." And still others objected to the use of the school-house for that purpose, and caused it to be locked up. The school was discontinued from Thanksgiving time to May for a number of years. From the time of shutting up the school-house, the Sunday-school was held in the meeting-house. With the females the school was more popular; aud during the first summer, more than seventy joined the school. Mrs. Sweetser, the manager and teacher of this department had the valuable services of other teachers, such as Patty Doty, afterwards Mrs. Abraham Wood, Mary Doty, afterwards wife of Rev. Joseph Wood, and Miss Olive Emery. A brother of Mrs. Sweetser, a very earnest Christian, started near the same time, the first Sabbath-school ever held in Fitchburg.

The first real *organization* of our Sunday-school was brought about by Mr. afterwards Rev. Dr. David O. Allen, in 1824, while acting as missionary of the American Sunday School Union. How long the males and females met in different rooms I do not know, but not probably after the males adjourned to the meeting-house. A great interest was taken in committing Scripture verses to memory; in some instances a hundred or more verses were learned each week by the young ladies. And the New Testament and Psalms were committed to memory in less than a year by one young lady in the village. This was doubtless carried to excess, and absorbed an undue amount of time and interest, to the neglect, perhaps, of carrying out in practice the injunctions learned.

In 1830, a Board of Managers were chosen, Mr. Mann being chosen President, and Dea. B. F. Wood, Superintendent. Dea. Aaron Wood was Superintendent, in 1832, 1833, and 1834. Dea. Sewall Barnes was Superintendent in 1835. That year the pastor was invited to preach a sermon upon Sabbath-schools which he did, and continued to do so from time to time. Other Superintendents, have been, Franklin Jones, Dea. Edward Kendall, Abner H. Merriam, George Kendall, W. S. Abbott, J. F. Clark, A. B. Holden, D. W. Hill, C. T. Damon, and T. D. Wood, the present Superintendent. Dea. W. S. Bradbury was for many years the very efficient secretary of the school, and used to make excellent annual reports to the local Conferences of churches. Committees were appointed, for many years, in each district to interest persons in attending the school: and the church as a body seemed to feel that the care of the school was committed to them; and from it have gone out a large number of persons who have held and who still hold high and honored positions in the various walks of life, and in the different spheres of duty. How pleasant it is after fifty years of labor in the Sabbath-school to look over its records and to read the names of those who have become leaders in all important spheres of life; physicians, lawyers, clergymen, representatives, senators, and governors; and above all to know that they are high-toned Christian men, and a blessing and an honor to society and the world. This school has reason to thank God that it has sent out such men, and also scores of others, who, though moving in the common walks of life, are nevertheless ornaments of society, and the trusted and true wherever their lot may be cast, reflecting the light shed upon their hearts from the instructions of faithful teachers in the Sabbath-school. And we will raise our memorial to-day in praise of that grace and love which has been Divinely shed upon us during the last half century. God bless our Sunday-school!

MISSIONARIES, AND THE MISSIONARY SPIRIT.

This church has shared largely in the missionary spirit; and in the reflex influence of sacrifices and consecrations which ever flow back in large measure to such churches or individuals as devote themselves to the work of missions.

This church was among the first in the State to adopt the missionary concert, held at first on the first Monday afternoon of each month; and it was even then largely attended, people leaving their work, though in the midst of haying time, to attend the meetings. In about 1830, the time was changed to the first Sabbath evening of each month, and has thus continued ever since. These concerts have been well sustained, and the collections have in some years amounted to upwards of fifty dollars. The American Board secured the warm and undivided sympathy of this church up to the year 1845; and from that time to the present, while contributing generously to that cause, she has sympathized more deeply with the American Missionary Society; and from its origin about that time, has contributed largely towards its support. The church has at different times during the last twenty-five years, been divided on these two causes, each having had its warm advocates; but from the strong anti-slavery sentiment in the church, the American Missionary Society, has shared more largely in the contributions and prayers of the people, than the

American Board, receiving some years of late five hundred and fifty dollars. So also the Home Missionary Society has shared in our sympathy and support; the Sunday-school Union, the Massachusetts Sabbath-school Society, the Home for Consumptives, the Home for Consumptives' Children, the Seamen's cause, Tract Society, Bible Society, the cause of Temperance,—have all of them received sympathy and aid from this church. The church has also supported altogether or in part, a teacher to the Freedmen of the South ever since the war; and she still continues her labors in that field with great success. Miss Martha L. Boutelle, the teacher referred to, is a member of the Congregational Church in Leominster, where her parents live; but she has many relatives and warm friends in this church. Hence her adoption by this society. Her fields of labor have been Washington, D. C., Hampton, Va., and Charleston, S. C., where she is now laboring. Her schools have elicited the warmest commendations from Gen. Howard of the Freedmen's Bureau. Enthusiastically devoted to her mission, with kindness of heart, a self-sacrificing spirit, and possessed of natural tact and spiritual fitness, she could not but accomplish a good work and bring much honor to Christ. Some fifteen or twenty members of this church have entered the ministry, besides nearly as many others who have become the wives of clergymen.

This church has also sent out a few of her number into the foreign missionary field. Miss Caroline Wood, daughter of Ezra Wood, married Rev. (now Dr.) Samuel Wolcott, of Cleveland, O., who with his wife served under the American Board, for a number of years in Turkey. Mary A. Sawyer, granddaughter of Rev. Mr. Rice, a former pastor, married

Rev. W. C. Jackson, a very successful teacher in the Academy in this town; and under whose labors an interesting religious awakening was enjoyed among the students. He and his wife consecrated themselves to the missionary work, and entered the Syrian field under the American Board of Commissioners for Foreign Missions, where they spent twenty full years of faithful and successful service for the Master. Since returning to their native land, Mr. Jackson has labored in guiding the flock of God in two or more places; his present field is in South Acton, where happiness and prosperity are crowning his efforts to do good. He and his excellent wife are remembered in this place with respect and love.

Rev. Dr. David O. Allen married Myra Wood, daughter of 'Squire Abel Wood, who, with her husband, sailed for India, June 6, 1827, three days after their marriage. Farewell services were held in the church on the Hill, Dr. Leonard Woods of Andover preaching the sermon. The occasion of their departure was very solemn and deeply interesting. Much prayer was offered, and many of the young people were deeply affected even to tears. When they looked her in the face for the last time, and saw her placid countenance, as calm as a summer's evening, and beaming with joy, they were forcibly impressed with the loftiness of her mission, and the reality of that religion which inspired and sustained her. The choir, of which she had been a leading member for seventeen years, were especially moved to tears. After her departure she wrote them an interesting and touching letter.

Upon her departure, a shower of Divine grace cheered and blessed the church, and the community; and as the result the church was greatly refreshed and enlarged, fifty-eight being added to it of fresh converts. Thus was happily fulfilled the words of sacred promise, "In watering others, ye shall be watered." Mrs. Allen lived in Bombay, India, the scene of their labors, about four years. She died after a few hours' sickness, and in the full triumphs of faith. And her precious dust hallows the far off field of India which she had chosen for the scene of her earthly labors.

Her memoir was written by her pastor, Rev. Mr. Mann, and passed through three or four editions; and was instrumental in quickening many churches in the missionary work. A sweet and lofty spirit, with good natural talents, a fine education, very devoted and full of self-denial, and entirely consecrated to her chosen work, she may well have looked forward to a happy and a useful life; but the ways of Providence are often inscrutable, and she was called away in the midst of her usefulness, and her hopes, mourned by a deeply stricken and a devoted husband, and by parents and a large circle of relatives and friends. Yet death but opened to her a brighter world of sweeter and unending service and joy. But in her death the church of which she was a member, was greatly blessed. In her it had an example of pure devotion, of noble ambition, of high resolve and lofty purpose; and her early death only heightened the missionary spirit in the church and community. A brief life nobly given up to such a cause, and accomplishing so much good teaches us that life is not to be measured by years, but by deeds and heart beats that throb for our fellow-men, and by sacrifices that exhibit the true spirit of Christ. The name of Myra Wood will ever be fragrant in the memory of all who knew her, or who knew of her lovely character or her heroic life. Truly, "the memory of the just is blessed." And if it seems sad to have our friends die among strangers, and in a foreign land, we may be consoled by the thought that—

> "Whether upon the gallows high
> Or in the battle's van,
> The proper place for man to die
> Is where he dies for man;"

and that the ascent of the spirit to the presence of the Savior can as easily be made from the wild jungles of India, as from Christian home or native soil.

Mr. Allen, the husband of Myra, moved by an urgent call for reinforcements for the foreign field, consecrated himself to the missionary work, and entered at once upon his life-mission. Newell, Nichols, Frost and Hall had deceased, and Nott and Bardwell had returned to this country. The dying appeal of Gordon Hall was not to be resisted, and starting for Calcutta he reached that port in September. Stopping a month there, he went to Bombay. He established the first missionary station in Ahmednugger, in 1831. Remaining there a few years, he next made extensive tours in Western India, preaching, and distributing Bibles, tracts, &c. In 1844 he took charge of the printing establishment in Bombay, where for ten years he performed a very important service in missionary operations. Dr. Allen was author of several very useful tracts in the Mahratta language. He also translated portions of the Old Testament, and superintended, and revised and corrected editions of the whole Scriptures into Mahratta. His health became impaired by too close study, and in 1853 he started for America, making a short stop in Palestine, and England, arriving in Boston in June. He soon after prepared the "History of India, Ancient and Modern," an octavo volume of six hundred pages, published in 1856,—a valuable history. He died a few years since, and no doubt has heard the "well done" from the Master. His was a life of high and holy consecration, and he is reaping his reward, where ties of friendship are renewed, and all love and joy are immortal.

PATRIOTISM.

The patriotism of this church and town, presents an unblemished record during its whole history, from the trying times of the Revolution, indeed, from the French and Indian War, more than a century ago, down to the close of the late Rebellion.

Soon after the act of incorporation into a town in 1770, the subject of resisting the encroachments of Great Britain became the absorbing theme. Westminster, though a little obscure town among the hills, took a deep interest in the contest. In February 11, 1773, they passed a resolution in town meeting, approving the opposition made by the citizens of Boston, to the unjust requisitions of the crown. In December, 1774, they passed a vote forbidding the constables to pay the money collected on the Province tax, to the treasurer appointed by the governor, and directing them to pay it to the treasurer, appointed by the people. At the same time they voted that they would support *their proportion of the poor of Boston*, in consequence of its occupancy by the emeny. At a town meeting held June 10, 1776, it was voted unanimously that if Congress would declare the Colonies Independent, they would support them with their lives and fortunes. During that war, Abner Holden, Nathan Wood and Joseph Miller represented the town in the General Court, and in the Congress that convened to deliberate upon the affairs of the nation.

Westminster, assured Samuel Adams "that she would join them in defence of our liberties, whenever an occasion should present itself." And on the 19th of April, 1775, on hearing of the march of the British troops, and of their outrage upon Lexington, the Westminster companies commanded by Captains Elisha Jackson, John Estabrook, and Noah Miles, marched immediately for the scene of action with more than fifty men. And in the Oration given at the celebration of our Soldiers' Monument, the present season, by Rev. Joseph Peckham, we were told that Westminster, with a population of eight hundred, furnished in all for the Revolutionary War, "three full companies of ninety men each." Col. Nicholas Dike became one of Gen. Washington's body-guard. And when a State Constitution was submitted to the people for acceptance or rejection, this town rejected it, setting forth as one reason among many others, "that it deprived a part of the human race of their natural rights, *on account of their color, which no power on earth has a right to do*." Thus early asserting the true doctrine of freedom and of human rights. The Constitution was rejected by the State; and when another and a better was submitted to the people, it was accepted, and Westminster gave her voice in its behalf.

It is worth while to mention the fact that Johnathan Minott from this place, was in the battle of Bunker Hill, and saw Gen. Warren when he fell; and his brother Joseph was accidentally shot in the same battle.

And that same spirit of patriotism which animated and fired the hearts of the early settlers of this town, has ever lived in their sons. And during the late civil and bloody war, this church and community have not lacked in devotion to the interests of their country; nor have they withheld their best blood and hard earned treasure from their country's altar, as yonder beautiful granite shaft most proudly tells; upon whose ample sides you may read the names of one hundred and thirty-two of your dearest kindred who fell in the defence of our liberties and for the severing of slavery's chain from the necks of four millions of God's children, our brethren. Your eyes may fill with affection's tears as you read their names, but your hearts will swell with a just pride that you and they were able to sacrifice so much for freedom's cause, and your country's weal. And furthermore, you have freely given, for the slave set free, garments for the naked, food for the hungry, and numberless comforts for the sick and dying of these sons of the night. With no grudging hand have you toiled and parted with your stores that the poor Freedmen might not perish; and with no less zeal than you prepared lint and bandages, and sick-room delicacies for the wounded soldiers in camp and hospital in the times of carnage that tried men's souls.

Now we rejoice in a conquered peace, in a country of true freedom, in the dawning light of justice and equality to all men white and black; and may no injustice ever again be built into this government, lest it prove to be the hay, wood, and stubble which in its purging will consume and cause to topple down the whole fabric of our nationality. A true patriotism will watch the interests, and seek the welfare of a nation in times of peace; and baptized in the spirit of true religion will insure peace, prosperity, and an honored life. And with New England's truest poet and the slave's best friend, we may say:

> "And now with slavery blotted out!
> All within and all about
> Shall a fresher life begin;
> Freer breathe the universe,
> As it rolls its heavy curse
> On the dead and buried sin."

ANTI-SLAVERY SENTIMENT.

This church has been radical on every reform that has agitated the country. To be sure when the subject of slavery was first agitated, like most other churches there was a holding back; but it was one of the first to wheel around right, and to espouse the cause of the oppressed in our land. In 1845 or the year following, when a separation took place between the radical and the conservative element in the American Board, resulting in the formation of the American Missionary Association, this church warmly sympathized with the latter, and has continued to do so until the present day. Among the many who advocated the Colonization theory, some were found in this church. But through the lectures of Mr. Weld, heard in Boston by some of our people, their minds were turned from the theory of Colonization to the true theory of Emancipation.

Sympathy for the oppressed was very strong, and efforts were made to indoctrinate the people in the true gospel of freedom. Among the leaders in this work, were Dea. Edward and George Kendall, Dea. Joel Merriam, Hon. Joel

Merriam, Jr., William Heywood, Dea. Robert Peckham, Dea. J. T. Everett, George Miles, Benjamin Wyman, Alfred Wyman, and Calvin Whitney. The following persons have lectured more or less in this town upon the subject: William Lloyd Garrison, Abby Kelly, the Misses Grimke of South Carolina, Sally Holly, and others. It was through the efforts of Dea. Peckham that a Mr. Goodyear was introduced to this place to lecture on the cause of the oppressed. He lectured in the Congregational Church, all day and evening, carrying with him the sympathy of the whole congregation with a very few exceptions. A society was soon formed as the result, as was done in most of the surrounding towns within a few months from that time. Dea. Peckham's house was the head-quarters for these lecturers, where they found a welcome, often a week at a time.

About this time, or a little after, Henry B. Stanton, a student of Dr. Lyman Beecher of Cincinnati, lectured here several days and evenings. Mr. Stanton, Theodore Weld, Mr. Dresser and several others left Mr. Beecher's Institution on account of the Faculty's prohibiting their action on the subject of anti-slavery. And full of fire they went forth to scatter broadcast the anti-slavery gospel. Mr. Stanton and Mr. Dresser, spent a week here, after their first visit. This Mr. Dresser was the one who was whipped by the decision of a citizens' court at Nashville, Tenn., because in going out to sell Bibles, he had put pamphlets between the leaves, and one on anti-slavery was found in his carriage. After his whipping, he fled, leaving all his effects behind him.

Mr. Torrey, who suffered martyrdom in a Maryland prison, was often here, besides several others who have suffered much in the cause. Dea. Peckham has several times sheltered under his roof, and fed from his table, and in other ways helped onward toward Canada the fleeing slave. At one time a Quaker late one Saturday night brought to his house a slave mother and child. The mother on being uncovered was found to be white, and the child only slightly tinged with color. She was delighted with her reception, and told the story of her escape. Collecting seven dollars for her, their benefactor directed the Quaker where to go in Gardner, the next night (Sunday); and with the fugitives all covered up in the carriage, on to freedom they wended their way, in sweet and glorious triumph! Thank God, *this* is now the land of true freedom!

About the time of the formation of the American Missionary Society in 1845-6, William Lloyd Garrison gave a number of lectures in this town, which aroused a good deal of feeling on the subject. He also introduced his paper, the Liberator, into many families. In this paper he took strong grounds against the church, as well as against slavery, and because it did not come up to his estimate of its duty; because it was indifferent towards, and in many cases opposed the great work that filled his heart, he looked upon it as false to its charge and as radically corrupt. Hence his invectives against it, and his little confidence in a religion that would treat with coldness a subject which in his view was the embodiment of all truth. Mr. Garrison was right in his views of the sin of slavery, and he was right in thinking that the church was too conservative on that subject; but he erred we think and did a good deal of harm by the bitterness with which he denounced the church, the ministry, and the Bible. And surely he had been wiser, and truer to that and to all truth, had he attempted a *cure* of the disease of the church, instead of seeking with impatience to destroy the church itself. The followers of Mr. Garrison were called "Garrisonians," and that portion of the church which followed his advice in leaving the church were styled " Come-outers ;" and among this latter class were a few in this town and in this church, while the church as a body may be considered as having sympathized deeply with the oppressed, so much so as to be called radical on the subject; yet they did not as a body think it necessary, in espousing the one cause to desert the other. But all evil that grew out of the efforts of Mr. Garrison to liberate the slave, are incidental, and transient ; and now that the " peculiar institution " has toppled down, and all the world are ready to be classed with the once " hated abolitionists," now a term of peculiar honor, we can afford to pardon any errors or excess of zeal in Mr. Garrison and his sympathizers. Surely there is quite a contrast between Mr. Garrison in 1832, led through the streets of Boston by a mob, with a halter around his neck, and Mr. Garrison in 1868, his great work accomplished, and receiving from the friends of freedom throughout the land, a golden memorial of fifty thousand dollars, for his untiring efforts in making freemen of millions of his fellow-men! In Bryant's noble words,

"Truth crushed to earth shall rise again ;—
The eternal years of God are hers."

TEMPERANCE.

The subject of temperance has been agitated in this town for more than forty years. In early days when it was customary to drink intoxicating liquors at ordinations, funerals, weddings, and at social gatherings, this town followed the fashion; and a pernicious fashion it proved to be for this community, since many drunkards were made, and for many years, the best part of our business men, were killed off by this ruthless demon.

The first open action taken in the matter, was the reading of Dr. Lyman Beecher's six sermons on Intemperance, before the congregation at intermission on the Sabbath. This was in 1828. And many other churches were doing the same thing. These sermons created a good deal of sensation and did much good. About that time a stand was taken by a successful attempt to raise the Academy building without liquors. A great triumph for those times. A temperance society was formed in town, by a few of Mr. Mann's people April 27, 1829, auxiliary to the American Temperance Society. With much difficulty, twelve members—the apostolic number—were obtained. Many were afraid to join "lest they should fail to obtain help to carry on their farms." About this time Mr. Mann received a commission from Dr. Woods of Andover, President of the American Temperance Society, to act as agent for the society in Worcester (North) County. Accordingly the temperance society in Westminster was remodelled on the principles of total abstinence, after many attempts for a long time to evade its adoption. Dea. Edward Kendall and Dea. Joel Merriam were warm and earnest advocates for the cause; so also was Dea. Peckham not a whit behind them. Other warm advocates of the cause were Dea. J. T. Everett, William Heywood, Dea. B. F. Wood, Dea. Murdock, Hon. Joel Merriam, Jr., Joseph and George Kendall, Dea. Barnes, and Dea. Aaron Wood. The following resolution, presented by Dea. Edward Kendall, was adopted by the church February 2, 1837:

"*Resolved* that in the opinion of this church, the use of all intoxicating liquors as a common drink, is immoral and sinful, and that such use by church members, is calculated to bring reproach upon the cause of religion."

Certainly a very strong, plain and conclusive statement; and one to which the church has ever since held allegiance; and nothing that can intoxicate has for a long time been used for sacramental purposes; and the leading members of the church are the leaders in the temperance cause, both in the open, and secret Temperance Societies in town. This cannot be said of too many Christian churches in the land. But the time, we trust, is coming when there will be as great a change of public sentiment on this subject as has been wrought on the subject of slavery, and in the same direction. God hasten the day!

ANTI-MASONRY.

Long before the anti-slavery, or the temperance agitation, the anti-Masonic movement was inaugurated; and it seemed more threatening of civil war than did either of the other agitations. This movement began in Western New York about the time of the alleged murder by the Masons of Morgan, who had revealed, in a book, the secrets of the Masonic order. The agitation soon spread all over the country. During all the excitement in New York, persons in this town were receiving anti-Masonic papers and pamphlets, in one of which a detailed account of the capture, confinement, and final disposal of Morgan was given.

There were some Masons in this town; and through the

efforts of Dea. Peckham, an anti-Masonic meeting was held to consider what measures should be taken to discourage the growth of the order. The deacon and Mr. Ezra Wood were appointed delegates to an anti-Masonic convention to be held in Worcester, subsequent to a State convention held in Boston for the same purpose. But the feeling against their going was so strong that they were persuaded not to attend. Dea. J. T. Everett, and Dea. Aaron Wood, and others interested themselves in this cause, deeming with others the Masonic influence baleful and subversive of the principles of republican institutions, as well as being anti-Christian.

John Quincy Adams was soon after put up as the anti-Masonic candidate for governor, and came near being elected. John Davis was elected by the Legislature, the people failing to elect either. The next year the Legislature passed a law prohibiting "all extra judicial oaths" under a heavy penalty; the result of which was that all the lodges in the State gave up their charters excepting the Grand Lodge, composed of the officers in all the other lodges. Whatever may be the merits or demerits of Free Masonry, it evidently meets a felt want of manifested *brotherhood*, which the church ought to meet and can, but does not to some in any satisfactory manner. If the church would discourage this Order let it cease bitter denunciation, and try to meet the want which that seems to supply in so good a degree.

It may not be known by all that *speculative* Free Masonry had its origin as late as 1717, in the Sun Tavern, London, England, though long before that there had been in that city societies for the different crafts, such as for carpenters, bakers, &c., and a society for co-operative masons; and for all the crafts there were rules for apprentices and for journeymen. Speculative Masonry in this country has of late received very great encouragement, and seems to be spreading more rapidly than ever. But whether with good reason or not, its growth is generally looked upon with suspicion if not with apprehension.

"PERFECTIONISM."

I have already alluded to the fact, that a change in doctrinal belief took place with quite a number of the leading members of this church during the last years of Mr. Mann's pastorate. I am unable to state the first or most important cause which inaugurated this change of sentiment. But I think it originated during a revival interest from the year 1837 to 1840, in which the several churches shared. At least the revival strengthened the doctrine. One of the Baptist preachers proved to be a "perfectionist." A Mr. Martin in 1842, or 1843 preached for Mr. Smith upon the subject; and at some time before or after this, a sermon on "perfection" by president Mahan of Oberlin College, was read by some, which had a powerful influence in confirming their minds in the doctrine of Christian Perfection. But whatever the immediate or remote causes, the fact was that quite a number of the prominent members of the church had embraced the doctrine, and were rejoicing in its blessings. This of course caused some excitement, and a division arose between the old school Calvinists and the Perfectionists who seem to have embraced this "distinguishing doctrine of Methodism." Some suppose this change of sentiment had something to do with the dismission of Mr. Mann. At least, upon his dismissal, the next pastor was a Perfectionist, Rev. S. S. Smith. And the result of the movement has been to bring about in the church a milder type of Calvinism, which is eminently new school, with two or three exceptional cases; and the Methodist element is quite largely predominant, though, at present there are but few who hold to the doctrine of "Christian Perfection," and they are all original converts.

The doctrine in question, "Perfect Love," "Holiness," "Entire Satisfaction," or Christian Perfection, is doubtless greatly misunderstood, and misrepresented. I will not attempt to give a definition of the doctrine lest I should fail to do justice to its advocates. It is defined by G. Peck, as "a distinct work wrought in the soul by the Holy Ghost;" by Bishop Hamline, as "specifically a new state, and not merely the improvement of a former state;" by Wesley, as "a second change, an instantaneous deliverance after justification, and not a gradual work." Persons professing to have passed through this experience, whatever it is, or is thought to be, express themselves as filled with love, and joy, and in some cases as living without sin for months and years; and hold that it is the privilege of all Christians thus to live always. Not that they cannot sin, or may not make mistakes, or may not err, but that they need not to live under condemnation. Now whatever be the truth or error of this doctrine, it has been believed by many of the very best members of this church, and is the distinguishing doctrine of the largest Protestant denomination in this country. And the Methodists are pioneers in the evangelization of the land. With their earnest piety, warm zeal, and genuine sympathy with the masses, and with their admirable system of church organization, perhaps on the whole the most effective system known, together with their views of free and full salvation for all, and their manifested spirit of friendliness and brotherly love,—the Methodists challenge the admiration of the world!

MEETING-HOUSES.

This church has had three meeting-houses. Almost the first thing thought of in the settlement of this town, was the rearing of a sanctuary for the worship of God. This was partly from religious motives, and partly as an inducement to persons to settle in such a wilderness, so far from civilization. And this shows how high an estimate our Puritan ancestors placed upon religious worship, and the uniting of religion with civil life. Their idea was to found a religious state, and this characteristic was for long seen in the settlement of new towns.

The site of the two first meeting-houses was on the "Hill" near the pond. The first church edifice was thirty-five by forty-five feet, and twenty feet posts. Dea. Joseph Miller was the master workman. At first there were no seats, then rough board seats, then when finished off, high box pews and lofty box pulpit, over which swung the sounding-board, such a terror to timid children, lest it should fall upon the minister's head. The seats of the pews were attached by hinges, so that when the people rose for prayers, the seats went up, and when they sat down, down went seats, "clatter, clatter," all over the house, and with tremendous noise. Stocks were kept under the pulpit for the unruly. The house having been finished on the outside, was dedicated June 6, 1739; sermon by Isaac Richardson of Woburn, from Haggai, ii. 9. A committee was annually chosen to "dignify and seat the meeting-house, according to rate (tax) and age," an important, but rather delicate duty, ending sometimes in squabbles in the church. The first church stood about forty-five years, when it was taken down to give place to a new one. It was then converted into a barn for the pastor Mr. Rice. Some of the timbers, sound as the hardest oak can be, are still in the barn frame of Mr. Raymond, the site of Mr. Rice's house.

The second meeting-house, was erected in 1788, and dedicated January 1, 1789. It was located on the hill a few feet back of the first church. It was sixty feet by forty-five feet, with box pews and galleries, and high pulpit; and in after years a tower or belfry was built on the west end ten feet square on the ground. There was an entrance in each end. A bell was secured by subscription. It was broken by having too heavy a tongue put in by advice of the maker, complaint having been made that the first tongue was too light. A second bell was secured and broken in the same way. When a third bell was talked of, many of the people wanted a society bell; but it was otherwise decided, after a good deal of contention; and to-day the bell belongs to the town. Mr. Norman Seaver fell from the frame of this second church, and was killed.

The third, and present meeting-house was dedicated January 3, 1837; the dedication sermon was by Rev. Mr. Mann, the pastor, from Haggai ii. 9: "The glory of this latter house shall be greater than of the former." The old church edifice was taken down, and the frame converted into a chair factory, called the "Old Red Mill," at the foot of Bacon street. The present meeting-house is eighty by fifty feet, and cost about seven thousand dollars. It was built by a corporation of twenty-six persons who took all responsibilities and ran all risks; and in selling the pews they realized several hundred dollars above cost, a rare occurrence. The vestry is underneath the church, and as in most similar cases, proves to be a great failure; the walls being constantly filled with dampness and covered with mould, endangering the health of persons sitting in it, in public gatherings of the church. Especially in the country, where land is cheap and abundant, vestries ought always to be built upon the ground, and if possible in the rear of the church, and communicating with it by doors on either side of the pulpit.

It was a great trial for some to give up the old "Hill," and come down to the village to worship. Nor is it strange, since for a full century the tribes had gone up that hill to pay their weekly devotions to God; and through the power of associations, it doubtless seemed to them that the spot was sacred, and the only "place where men ought to worship."

STOVES IN THE CHURCH.

As with all other churches, there were no stoves used in the church in this town until comparatively a recent period. There never was a fire lighted in the first meeting-house, nor in the second one until January 1, 1827. A period of ninety-two years had passed before it was ever conceived that a fire could be had in the church of God. How they kept warm we find it hard to conceive. But families used to go, the children as well as others, and they had to listen to sermons an hour long at least. Of course they braced themselves up to it as they had done to the endurance of many hardships. And during services there was not only music by the chilling winds that howled and surged upon the church, as on wintry days it swept across the hill with fury; but a sub-base was continually kept up by the stamping of feet on the floor, and the knocking of toes against the sides of the big, high pew. However good the long sermon might be, coming to the ear through so much frost, it chilled rather than warmed the heart. Surely to most the sweetest sound heard, must have been the "Amen" that saved them from freezing. And notwithstanding all this discomfort, when at length it was proposed by some to furnish stoves and fuel to warm up the church, the society voted not to accept the offer. And when in 1827 it was decided to have stoves, the vote was a bare majority, so fearful were they that the church would be burned up. And then it was a new thing, and conservatism looked upon it as a kind of innovation, and bordering on secularizing the church. And it would not be strange if some thought that it would tend to make it too easy and pleasant a thing to go to church. The stoves were obtained by subscription, through the efforts of Mr. Mann. And for a long time they were a terrible eyesore to some, who would imagine that they heard the roar of the fire consuming the church. At one time a person threw off his coat and made other demonstrations suggestive of excessive heat, when lo, no fire had been kindled that day! Our greatest trouble now is to keep warm enough.

CLOSING REMARKS.

But your patience has been put to a severe test,—quite as severe as was that of our fathers and mothers who listened to ordinary sermons,—and I must hasten to a close, with many things unsaid, and perhaps with some that had better been unsaid. But I have endeavored to be faithful, just, and kind.

And in this review, how are we struck with the power and grandeur and sublimity of the religion of Christ, and of the church of the living God! Surely the influence of the church can never be known in time. Its lines stretch out beyond mortal ken, observed only by the eye of the Omniscient. Who can measure the good done, even by this church! To know it, in anything like its full measure and meaning, we must know the spiritual history of some twelve hundred members for four or five generations, who in themselves and their descendants, have impressed their lives upon the world. The existence of a true church in a community is a great power for good. There are a thousand influences which gather around the Sanctuary and the Sabbath, and the ordinances of the church, which mould the heart and shape the life beyond what can possibly be known. The sound of the Sabbath bell calling to worship, the spire pointing upward to the heavens;—all these things are a power for good to arrest the careless, and to remind all that there are interests concerning them which pertain to the life to come.

Throughout an entire century and a quarter, this church has not been without a meeting-house, or a preached gospel; and many times has it been crowned with the richest tokens of God's grace and mercy, in religious awakenings. Not without its imperfections, and its errors, or its trials, this church has had a remarkable history, and one in very large measure, creditable and honorable. It has been strong and stable, and for many years was the leading church in this part of the county, and possessed considerable influence abroad. At an early period of its history it contained between four and five hundred members, and was then the largest country church in the State. Foremost and earnest in espousing the cause of the oppressed, it has not withheld sympathy from any reforms of the day. And its spirit of liberality has far exceeded its means to contribute to all good objects.

This church has always respected the independency of the pulpit, and the proper dignity of the ministerial office. And while radical and progressive in the outward labors and reforms, it exhibits signs of a progressive spirit in the domain of religious truth, and in the realm of theologic enquiry. It regards those as not enquiring wisely who contend that the old paths are better than the new. And as we take a retrospective view to-day, and set up our memorial, we but confess that we are not yet through the wilderness, and that the battles are not all fought, and the advancement not all made. Forward, and ever onward, is to be our watchword until we reach the goal, and receive the crown.

Progress in the *improvement* of *truth* there may not be, there is not needed; all truth is eternal and does not admit of improvement; but there is such a thing as *progress in theology;* progress in the interpretation, the development and application of truth, and the banishing of error from the head and heart; progress in meeting the wants of an advancing age, and the varying needs of the human soul. A correct belief is valuable, but only as it is made to minister to the growth of true piety and the enlargement of the spirit of charity and love; *fidelity in duty* being the true test of a religious life. And as progress is made in the right direction, the church will become pure and holy, and full of charity and religion will be a power in the earth for good, and Christ and God will be enthroned in the heart and life.

A *practical* religion is the demand of the age ; a religion that is worshipful, but which has especially to do with this lower world, and our relations with our fellow-men ; that, like leaven permeates all life and labor, and hallows every thought, word and deed, making men pure and true and noble, and manly, and thus fitting them for heaven.

A *cheerful* religion, full of warmth and sunlight, of charity and benevolence, of hope and sweetness, is demanded, and is alone of kinship with the spirit of the Master. It is high time that cant and whine, and gloomy faces, and whatever caricatures the blessed religion of Christ, were ostracized, and banished from every heart, home and sanctuary in the wide world! Our watch-word must be *forward;* and we are to forget all past victories or defeats, and to reach forward to the things before, and above us. And this spirit of progress, of a thoroughly radical and reformatory religion, is in exact harmony with Congregationalism, and the teachings of our Puritan fathers. Their words were, "the Lord has more truth yet to break out of His holy word." They were not shut up to any letter or creed theology. Theirs was "liberty for making great changes of opinion and practice, should fresh light break forth upon them," according to their own words. And shall ours be a less liberal, a less progressive, a less tolerant faith? But in reaching forward, let us gather up and carry along with us all of the past which has in it truth and goodness, avoiding this blind veneration of the past merely because it is not new. All truth is not in the past ; it is to be gathered each day as we tread life's pathway, fresh and suited to the times, and the wants of the human heart.

A right Christian life here is the only guaranty of a happy hereafter; and the degree of holiness in the present life ; the real attainments here in a pure and a true Christian *character,* will determine the degree of happiness in the great future. The future is in an important sense *a continuation of the present life;* and the soul carries with it into the spirit world all its accumulations, and its amount of culture acquired in its earthly experience.

What we need, then, is *soul-culture,* a right life inspired and aided by faith in God, and love and obedience to Christ, and love to our fellow-men. What we need is the *Truth;* that alone saves ; not dead dogmas, or a dead orthodoxy, but *vitalized truth,* that makes men better, happier, holier ; that in fitting them for this life, prepares them for the future ; that in carrying us onward, lifts us upward to a true immortality.

And now in view of what God has wrought for us as a church ; in view of the toils, self-denials and prayers of the pious dead, who have given to us the heritage of a pure religion ; in view of a prosperous present, and a hopeful future, are we not called upon in setting up to-day our stone of help, to renew our covenant vows, and *to rededicate ourselves to the unfinished work before us!*

We are compassed about to-day with a great cloud of witnesses. Not only the living, but the spirits of the departed are looking down upon us. May we not believe that Marsh, and Rice, and Mann, with dear and blessed memory are interested in this occasion, and in the future welfare of this church ? most surely they are, as are all the pious dead of our number who sing in glory. Then let us run the race with patience, looking unto Jesus the author and finisher of our faith. Let us grasp with firm hand and brave heart, the banner of the cross, and bear it forward with heroic zeal, until it shall be planted in all lands, and the kingdoms of this world shall become the kingdoms of our Lord and Saviour. Let us march on through life's wilderness, trusting in Israel's God, until the heavenly Canaan shall gladden our vision, and in triumph, we can say in the " Better Land," "*Hitherto hath the Lord helped us!*"

APPENDIX.

ORDER OF PROCEEDINGS.

At a meeting of the Congregational Church, in Westminster, in March, 1868, it was voted to celebrate the One Hundred and Twenty fifth Anniversary of the Organization of the Church, and the following persons were chosen a Committee to make all necessary arrangements for the occasion, viz:

Dea. David W. Hill,	Dea. T. D. Wood,	Rev. A. J. Rich.
Mrs. J. B. Wood,	Mrs. Benson Bigelow.	

At a subsequent meeting of the Church, it was voted to invite the pastor, Rev. A. J. Rich, to prepare a discourse for the occasion, and to secure a poem and hymns. The following Committee on Correspondence was also chosen:

Dea. Robt. Peckham,	Dea. B. F. Wood,	Jonas Miller,
J. B. Wood,	Dea. T. D. Wood,	Dea. D. W. Hill,
Asa Cutting,	Rev. A. J. Rich,	Dr. Clinton Warner.

Also, a Committee on Decoration, as follows:

Mrs. Augustine Whitney,	Miss Hattie Minott,	Mrs. Maria Whitney,
Mrs. Jennie Burgess,	Miss Lucy Wright,	Mrs. Wallace Cheney,
Mrs. Stedman Morse,	Mrs. Stillman Whitney,	Miss Ellen Wright,
Mrs. A. E. Drury,		

Mr. Arba Pierce, Church decorator, whose services were highly appreciated by the other members of the Committee.

Committee on Providing and Distributing the Collation:

Dea. and Mrs. D. W. Hill,	Mr. and Mrs. Stillman Whitney,
Dea. and Mrs. T. D. Wood,	Mr. and Mrs. Augustine Whitney,

Mr. and Mrs. A. B. Holden,
Mr. and Mrs. Benson Bigelow,
Mr. and Mrs. J. B. Wood,
Mr. and Mrs. T. S. Wood,
Mr. Charles T. Damon,
Mr. and Mrs. William Mayo,
Mr. and Mrs. Wallace Cheney,
Mrs. John Sawin,
Mr. Franklin Lombard,
Mr. L. Hartwell,
Mr. Edward Miller,
Mr. Frederick Minott,
Mrs. W. Benjamin,

Mr. Augustus Eager,
Mr. and Mrs. Stedman Morse,
Mr. and Mrs. Noyes,
Mrs. Edward Bacon,
Mrs. Sawtelle,
Mrs. Underwood,
Mrs. Kate Baker,
Mr. Luke Divol,
Mr. C. F. Merriam,
Miss Jennie Brown,
Mrs. J. T. Everett,
Miss Sarah Hardy,
Miss Lizzie Whitney.

The following were chosen as ushers to assist Mr. G. W. Gibbs, the sexton, in seating the people:

Frank Wood, Frederick Gibbs, Stillman Whitney.
Myron Sawin,

The day for the Celebration came in cloudy, and its threatening aspects prevented many from coming from a distance; but it was a very comfortable day, and it did not rain till evening. The church was filled to overflowing at 10 o'clock, the hour appointed for the Celebration, at which time the services commenced. The following order of exercises was issued, and scattered through the audience:

ORDER OF EXERCISES.

MORNING.

VOLUNTARY—ANTHEM.

INVOCATION, ... *By Rev. Dr. L. Sabin.*
HYMN, ... *Words by Mrs. M. A. Burrage.*

THE CHURCH'S CALL.

The day of our reunion,
  The day we celebrate
Is calling to communion,
  Our sons in every State,
We hail with joy and gladness,
  Our Church's natal day,
Though not unmixed with sadness,
  Our mind will backward stray—

To days of pain and sorrow,
  To days of labor,—toil;
To thoughts of what the morrow
  Might bring, their work to foil;
To where the Indian prowler,
  And wily beasts of prey,
Lay wait, like many a fowler,
  The unwary to betray.

'Twas in such days of hardship,
  This corner-stone was laid,
That we their sons might worship,
  With none to make afraid.
Shall we the humble offspring
  Of such a noble sire,
Refuse to lay our offering
  Upon their altar's fire?

We hasten at your bidding,
  We give you hearty cheer.
Gladly the bond cementing
  Of Christian Union dear.

Once more in concert bending,
  Around the Throne of Grace,
To God our souls commending
  In our *dear native place*.

Let dews of grace come o'er us,
  In sweet refreshing showers;
Bring heavenly scenes before us,
  In these our festal hours;
And let each prayer ascending,
  A gracious answer bring;
While we our voices blending,
  Adore our Heavenly King.

READING OF THE SCRIPTURES AND PRAYER, *By Rev. M. Ames.*

HYMN—"COME THOU FOUNT."

HISTORICAL DISCOURSE, . . . *By Rev. A. Judson Rich, the Pastor.*

PRAYER, ... *By Rev. M. H. Hitchcock.*

HYMN, ... *Words by Mrs. Sarah Hubbard.*

A century and a quarter spanned,
  Since in this sacred place,
A little consecrated band,
  Were led by sovereign grace.

Revered that band who planted here
  The Cross, to rally round;
And gathered in this sunniest spot,
  A church,—'tis holy ground.

Our infant feet once trod these courts,
  Here learned to lisp Thy praise;
Here consecrated at the font,
  In early halcyon days.

A scattered band return to-day,
  To filial, waiting arms;
Your mandate, so replete with love,
  Brought with it many charms.

The spire that lifts its towering hight
  Above the village green;
Seems radiant with a burnished light,
  Beckoning us home again.

Where are our sires whose living voice
  Once echoed back our call?
Will they not list while we rejoice,
  In raptures, one and all?

We love their mem'ry, love their deeds,
  We praise their Christian lore;
And to their prayers our minds gave heed,—
  Their God will we adore.

BENEDICTION.

RECESS—COLLATION IN TOWN HALLS.

AFTERNOON.

ANTHEM—"I AM THE ROSE OF SHARON."

HYMN, ... *Words by Mrs. M. A. Burrage.*

THE CHURCH'S WELCOME.

Welcome, neighbors, welcome townsmen,
  Dwelling far away, or near;
Welcome, Christian friends and kinsmen,
  To you all a hearty cheer!

Welcome, Christian fathers, mothers,
  Children of the sainted dead;
Welcome, Christian sisters, brothers,—
  Welcome to this Church of God.

Welcome to this pleasant township,
  Where our honored fathers dwelt;
Welcome to this Church—ay, worship
  At the altar where they knelt,—
At the altar where, in childhood,
  You the seal of God received;
Where, in after youth or manhood,
  You confessed that you believed.

May the mantles of the fathers,
  Which, in dying, they laid down,
Be bequeathed to sons and daughters
  Of this goodly church and town;

May we neither pause nor falter,
  Or the cause of God disclaim;
But beneath His sacred altar,
  Gather strength to bear His name.

May this day of our reunion
  Be a day of joy and love;
Be a day of sweet communion
  With the saints below, above;
That when we are called to sunder
  Ties that bind us here on earth,
We may rise with that blest number,
  To a new and Heavenly birth.

PRAYER.

ORIGINAL HYMN, ... *By Miss M. E. Whitney.*

Our fathers' God, Thy little flock
  Long hast Thou watched in love;
And wilt Thou still in mercy look
  Upon us from above.

Upon these hills hath brightly beamed
  The glory of the Lord;
The rays of heavenly light have streamed
  Upon us from Thy word.

May we the light receive, and ne'er
  From duty turn aside;
Help us the cross Thou giv'st, to bear,
  O Thou, the Crucified!

Though resteth not on human brow
  The Pentecostal flame,
Love's fire should glow within us now,
  While we adore Thy name.

    Our fathers' God, keep us from sin;
      As Thou hast watched o'er them,
    Lead us, till all are gathered in
      The New Jerusalem.

ADDRESSES TO THE SUNDAY-SCHOOL, { *By Rev. Marcus Ames, Rev. Wm. Belden, and Dea. B. F. Wood.*

SUNDAY-SCHOOL ANNIVERSARY HYMN.
                                        Words by Calvin Whitney, Esq.

E'er yet the Nineteenth Century's hand,
  Hath gleaned the fruitage of the land,
To place before the garner door
  Of Heaven's increasing golden store,—

We rise to lift our hearts in praise,
  For Sunday-schools' illumined rays;
We grateful pause at fifty rolls
  Of annual blessings on our souls.

Our fathers fed the lambs of old.—
  We'll keep them safe within the fold;
For still their hearts a token bear,
  Of God's eternal love and care

And when the Century's ripened field
  Of early piety revealed,
Leans to the reaper's sickle blade,
  The yielding fruits these schools have made;

    We'll praise anew, in gladder strains,
      The Eternal Father's hallowed name;
    And bless the reconciling love,
      That sent our Saviour from above.

REMARKS BY STRANGERS AND THE READING OF LETTERS,
    IN RESPONSE TO SENTIMENTS OFFERED.

HYMN—"ALL HAIL THE POWER OF JESUS' NAME."

PRAYER.

BENEDICTION.

EVENING—SOCIAL REUNION.

ADDRESSES, ... { *By Rev. Marcus Ames, Deacons Edward Kendall, N. H. Cutting, J. T. Everett and Moses H. Wood.*

CLOSING ADDRESS, ... *By the Pastor.*

PARTING HYMN—"BLEST BE THE TIE THAT BINDS."

BENEDICTION.

"GOD BLESS OUR CHURCH."

———o———

The following sentiments were read at the Celebration, and responded to for the most part by the persons whose names follow:

1. *The Founders of this Church*—Tried men and true—their courage was equal to their hardships, their faith to the greatness of their endeavors; may we, their sons, imitate their valor. [By Dea. B. F. Wood and Jonas Miller.]

2. *The Early Pastors and Deacons*—May their long and faithful services be a lesson of encouragement to those who may follow them. [Response by L. Sabin, D. D.]

3. *The Puritan Fathers*—Unswerving in their fidelity to God, and the principles of soul-liberty—may we never forget the debt of gratitude which New England and the world owes to them. [By Rev. A. P. Marvin.]

4. *The Christian Church*—The handmaid to Civil Liberty, and the truest exponent of a just Freedom.

RESPONSE BY LETTER FROM GOVERNOR BULLOCK.

BOSTON, September 7, 1868.

My Dear Sir:—I pray you to accept my most cordial thanks for your kind favor of the 29th August, inviting me to be present, on the 9th instant, at the observance of the one hundred and twenty-fifth anniversary of the organization of the Congregational Church in Westminster. My official engagements, already made for that day, must keep me away from your exercises; and nothing else would.

I recall, with vivid delight and freshness, the months of my youth passed in your ancient and beautiful town. I remember the good old church where I worshiped, guided by the dear and excellent pastor, Mr. Mann; his family, in which I boarded; all the hill-sides and fields where I roamed; the Academy and its bell, which summoned me to duty; the people of that day, also, I recall; now, alas, mostly gone from the scenes of the living. But, thanks to Heaven, your town lives; the church lives; the cause of education, truth, and morals lives, and will live through the eternal years of God. I wish I could unite with you in commemorating this anniversary day, but I cannot. My heart, however, will be in your midst, and in all your exercises. Believe me, my dear sir, most truly and faithfully, your friend and servant,

ALEX. H. BULLOCK.

THE REV. A. J. RICH.

5. *Christian Unity*—Like the Iris which spans Niagara, uniting, by a cord of light, two diverse nations,—may its hallowing and transforming power bind all Christian hearts into one glowing service of love, and thus fulfill the Savior's prayer, "*that they all might be one.*"

6. *Absent members and ex-members of the Church*—Their record is honorable, and their number large, scattered over all parts of the country, from Wachusett to the Nevadas, from the bleak hills of Worcester North, to the sunny, golden shores of the Eldorado.

LETTER FROM GEORGE WOOD, ESQ., OF CHICO, CAL.

NEW YORK, August 14, 1868.

My Dear Sir:—I regret my health and engagements forbid my acceptance of your kind invitation to participate in your proposed ceremonies, in celebrating the natal day of the Congregational Church of Westminster, of which you are pastor, and whose records embrace the names of so many who, being dead, yet *speak* to us through loved and cherished memories; and of not a few who were the beloved associates of my early life. The event will be one deeply interesting to every Christian heart, which can trace lineage to those venerated ancestors, who trod the stage of active life one hundred and twenty-five years ago, and who founded the church whose history you meet to recount.

My first recollections of life are associated with the spacious, old "meeting-house," on the hill, its capacious, square pews, with their uncushioned, and noisily rattling seats, the uncarpeted floors, the long choir of singers, whose faces are daguerreotyped on my memory, the cheerful Sabbath bell, inviting to worship, and its death knell, whose dirge-tone still sounds in memory's ear. No wintry blast was so piercing, and no snows so deep, as to prevent attendance at the Sabbath service, listening to the lessons of theological doctrine, or pastoral precept, from our revered pastor—while, in boyish ignorance, I feared the fall of the ponderous "sounding-board," apparently unsafely suspended over his devoted head. But no sermon was so eloquent, and no anthem so melodious, as to inspire my youthful heart with religious zeal, sufficiently fervid, on those wintry Sabbaths, in a fireless building, poised on the bleak hill-top, to withstand the intense cold. With shivering limbs and chattering teeth, summoning fortitude for endurance, we awaited the tardy Amen. Though stoves and carpets, at that day, would have been deemed a desecration of the house of God, the desire, nevertheless, *would* be often indulged, and sometimes cautiously *expressed*, that we might enjoy such sinful church luxuries.

To no spot of earth does the heart of the native New Englander cling with such tenacity, as to the blue hills among which he passed his childhood and youth. If educated and trained in accordance with the Christian principles of our beloved forefathers, his influence, in whatever sphere the wise Providence of God assigns him, will be wide-spread and healthful, restraining vice and ungodliness, winning men from sin to holiness, and dissipating evil from the orbit in which he moves, as the morning sun scatters the noxious vapors of the night. Many names, which will be suggested by this occasion, awaken reminiscences which rise, as sweet incense, in our retrospection, or as the aroma of faded flowers, which dying, leave their fragrance upon the air.

Around the teachings of our pastors, from the pulpit of the village "meeting-house," the lessons of rote, or oral instruction, in the Sabbath school, the prayers we learned to lisp at our mother's knee, and the thousand incidents and recollections associated with the district school-house of olden time, there clusters a host of pleasing memories, sacred and sweet to every New England heart; and one who could forget or despise *these*, casts away a treasure of more worth than gold, and proves himself unworthy his ancestral record.

Without the church and its kindred agencies, man would and *does* (as my observation bears testimony) soon relapse into a state of semi-barbarism. Were worldly considerations, temporal prosperity *alone*, to be consulted, the influence of the Christian Church and its associations would be a most powerful agency, in attainment of the desired object. But far higher, holier and more ennobling is the mission of the organization you celebrate, and whose history is stamped with so many chapters of thrilling interest to its surviving members. Of all the institutions of our age, the church and school-house stand out most prominently on life's canvas, and wield the most potent influence in moulding society, and ameliorating the condition of degenerate humanity. Truly blessed of God are those who have enjoyed the benefits of these institutions, under the favoring influences of our native land. The seed sown by your church and Sabbath-school, though sometimes long in germinating, has sprung up and borne fruit on the soil of nearly every nation, some already matured, and gathered by the Lord of the Vineyard, while other is now ripening for the harvest. You meet to commemorate an event dear to every son of Westminster, whose heart is enlisted in the cause of Christ, an organization, the influence of which will extend through all the cycles of eternity. Great is the responsibility of those who have been blessed with the influences and associations of New England institutions, and especially the church and Sabbath-school. "God works in a mysterious way," and often leads us in paths we know not. Thus I, in common with many who were nurtured as lambs of the flock, have gone out from your fold, to traverse pastures, wild and dreary, and crop spiritual herbage, unwatered by such dews as moisten the green soul-pastures of our "Faderland," or such rills as swell the still waters beside which *your* flocks are led.

Though thirty-six years a wanderer in distant lands, the memory of early days and sanctuary privileges is sweet, and when far removed from friends, and associations so dear to me in early life, my heart has often been saddened at the recollection of those songs of Zion, so fondly cherished by the Christian sons of New England. Such memories are as "apples of gold in pictures of silver," as choice gems set in the binding of life's history.

Sojourning in Southern climes, where "every prospect pleases, and only man is vile," and on the western verge of the American continent, where "sunny fountains roll down their golden sands," and "the heathen, in his blindness, bows down to wood and stone," my heart has clung to the sweet memories which cluster around the modest church spire of old Westminster. Far distant from the loved and cherished scenes of childhood and youth, Christian friends and associates of early life, witnessing scenes and conditions of society, which cause the Christian heart to bleed with anguish, the institutions under which I was reared have, year by year, gained a stronger hold on my affections, and I thank God, I had my birth and education within sound of the "church-going bells" of New England. No time or distance has sundered or can weaken the tie which binds me to the community in which I was nurtured, the church, within whose walls I first listened to the gospel invitation and the wonders of redeeming love, heard the first melodious strains of sacred song, and tasted the bread of life. *There*, are the graves of many who were dear to me. *There*, repose the ashes of my parents, around which memory lingers with an earnestness of devotion, none but an orphaned heart can comprehend.

Would you realize the value of the religious, social and literary privileges, with which God has blessed your people, go with me to the Pacific slope, and visit the aborigine, in his degradation and ignorance; the Chinese, bowing down to his idols, even under the waving folds of the "star spangled banner;" the Mexican, adhering to a *form* of Catholicism, but groping in darkness as truly heathen as that which enshrouds the pagan sons of China. Turn from these to the masses of adventurers of other nationalities, who seem to have forgotten that God rules; witness the great number whose names appear on the rolls of the Gospel army, and even those who have officiated as "watchmen on the walls of Zion," who, having assumed the garb of disloyalty, cast aside the insignia of the Cross. When you note how few observe, even the *outward* forms of vital piety, how sparsely are scattered over the land, temples consecrated to the worship of the true God, how wide-spread is the reign of infidelity in its most fascinating and delusive forms, and how opposed to true and undefiled religion is the great social voice of the country, you will be awakened to a deeper sense of the superior blessings God has showered upon your people. The Great Shepherd has graciously blessed the flock entrusted to your care in times past. May He bless *them* and *you* still *more* abundantly in the future. However widely scattered in our earthly pilgrimage, may we be reunited in the mansions of our Lord and Master, when our work is done and we shall have passed the portals of death, is the earnest desire and prayer of Yours, very affectionately, GEO. WOOD.

REV. MR. RICH, *Pastor of Congregational Church, Westminster, Mass.*

7. *Members of the Church, who have entered the Ministry*—May they be true to principles received in early life, and advance with the onward march of thought and truth. [Rev. Henry Cummings.]

8. *Education—the true handmaid to Religion*—May they ever walk together in mutual helpfulness. [Rev. Abel Wood.]

9. *The Cause of Temperance*—An interest which should lie near the heart of every lover of his kind,—this church, one of the first to move in the matter in this County, or the State, has ever since been loyal to the cause. [Dea. J. T. Everett, Amos B. Holden.]

10. *The Missionary Spirit*—This church has shared largely in it; may it continue to characterize it, until Christ shall reign from sea to sea, and from land to land. [Rev. M. H. Hitchcock.]

11. *Patriotism*—A part of every true religion; inbred in the sons of Westminster, whose fathers left these old hills to fight for their liberties in the Revolution, fighting at Bunker Hill, and in every campaign of the war, and whose sons laid down their lives for the deliverance of the land from the curse of slavery; may we emulate their valor, by a just appreciation of our liberties, and a readiness ever to answer to our country's call. [A. B. Holden, J. H. Miller.]

12. *The Philanthropic Spirit*—This church was always foremost in advocating the rights of the oppressed; and even have dared to harbor the fleeing slave under their roofs; but now, thank God, slavery is to be known among us no more forever. [Dea. R. Peckham, Dea. Edward Kendall.]

13. *The Future of this Church*—May its course be like the path of the just, shining "more and more unto the perfect day." [Rev. M. Ames, Deacons T. D. Wood, Frederick Whitney.]

14. *The Church and Pastor*—Whose memories to-day are so truly precious —whose star is in the ascendant; may their future be as *Rich* in faith and love as the past has been blessed and glorious.

(A voluntary—and responded to by the reading of an original Poem by the Pastor.)

15. *The Ladies of Westminster*—Daughters of noble mothers, are as beautiful and helpful as their fathers and brothers have been brave and loyal.

16. *The Choir*—Always noted for talent and unity—may it ever be a valuable aid to divine worship in this house of God. [Response by G. F. Miller, Esq., and a Song.]

17. *The Universalist Society*—Dissenting from her mother in doctrinal belief, yet one in all practical duties; may they unitedly labor for the advancement of all moral reforms, and mutually strive to promote harmony and brotherly love, which in itself is lovely, and a bond of perfectness.

RESPONSE BY REV. MR. PROCTOR (UNIVERSALIST).

The sentiment to which I am called upon to respond is very good. I am very much pleased with it. It is *peculiarly* RICH. It breathes a social, generous and noble spirit. It also breathes the spirit of the true mother. And I know of no spirit to which we poor, faulty creatures of earth are subject, more beautiful, affectionate or ardent than that of the pure and true mother. And I confidently hope and trust that the *daughter*, though herself far advanced in years—having long since passed the "critical thirtieth," and though wayward enough to dissent even widely from the time-honored theological views of the venerable mother—may yet work kindly, harmoniously and affectionately, "hand in hand," for the promotion and accomplishment of all those great and important social, intellectual and moral reforms and duties in which the respective parishes, and the community at large, have a common interest.

We all understand perfectly that no great and important enterprise is successfully accomplished in these modern times without combined effort, associated action. All societies calling themselves Christians, however widely they may differ in theology, should work together harmoniously, earnestly and persistently for the advancement of all those practical duties which beautify and bless the community, commonwealth and country.

The cause of Temperance is perhaps, at present, the greatest and most essential reform agitating the public mind; and for this reform we should all work in faithfulness and love. While it is my privilege to remain here as pastor of the Universalist Society, and in behalf of which I now speak, I will aim to work harmoniously with the other pastors, and have my people work thus with the other parishes in this beautiful hill-town, for the promotion of those practical interests which shall render our people prosperous, united and happy.

18. *The Baptist Society*—The youngest of the family; may the relations which exist between parent and child ever be those of mutual helpfulness, kindness and brotherly love. [Rev. R. G. Johnson, Baptist.]

A few of the sentiments were responded to in the evening, and some for want of time were omitted.

LETTER FROM REV. MR. BULLARD.

ROYALSTON, September 3, 1868.

Dear Brother:—Yours of August 31, inviting me to be present on the occasion of the Anniversary of the Church in Westminster, is received. Prior arrangements, which I cannot cancel, will call me to Amherst on the 9th, and oblige me, I am sorry to say, to forego the pleasure it would afford me to be with you.

I have pleasant recollections of the Rev. Cyrus Mann, the Church, and the Sabbath-school in Westminster, dating back to my college days, when I spent a winter as a teacher in one of your schools, and *went up* to the house of the Lord (on Sabbath days), as it then stood on high, and battled with the winds and snows of a severe winter. But the ancient house was filled with intelligent and earnest worshipers; and they had rich and faithful gospel sermons to feed upon. I was glad to renew my acquaintance with the pastor and the people, upon the commencement of my ministerial labors at Fitchburg, in 1837—an acquaintance which has not ceased until now; and has given rise to not a few grateful memories of occasions, families, and persons, all centering in your church.

Trusting your anniversary will prove an occasion of much solid pleasure and profit, and with sentiments of fraternal and Christian interest for the present pastor and membership of the Church in Westminster, I remain, dear brother, yours very truly, E. W. BULLARD.

REV. MR. RICH.

LETTER FROM CYRUS S. MANN, M. D.

PITTSFIELD, September 8, 1868.

My Dear Sir:—A somewhat severe illness, which has kept me in bed for several days, and from which I am only partially recovered, must be my excuse for not accepting your kind invitation to be present on Wednesday, at your celebration of the One Hundred and Twenty-fifth Anniversary of the Church and Society of which my honored father was, for more than twenty-six years, the minister. A thousand pleasant, sad, and holy memories crowd my mind, and I shall be with you in spirit, if not in person. My neighbor here, Moses H. Wood, a Westminster man, who is the present Superintendent of the Sabbath-school to Rev. Dr. Todd's Church, will respond for me, if there is any occasion. Accept my best wishes that the occasion may prove, as I doubt not it will, one of much pleasure and profit. I hope the young people will agree to observe, twenty-five years hence, the One Hundred and Fiftieth Anniversary; that we may all understand that henceforth, on the anniversary of each quarter of a century, looking out upon the grand old summits of Wachusett and Monadnock, the people of our Church and Society will lift up their voices in an anthem of grateful recollection to Him who has made and has kept it a blessing to the town, the county, the state, and the world. I am, sir, very sincerely and truly yours, CYRUS S. MANN.

REV. A. J. RICH.

LETTER FROM J. RUSSELL GAUT.

PHILADELPHIA, September 5, 1868.

My Dear Brother Hill:—Your kind letter inviting me to be present at the Anniversary of the Old Westminster Church, on the 9th inst., was duly received. I had already had notice of the same, with a pressing request to be present, from my mother and sister, and had hoped, up to a late hour, to be able to be present. I find, however, at this writing that it will be utterly impossible to do so. I regret it the more, not only because of the many familiar faces I shall thus fail to see, but the many *pleasant memories*, as well as *sad ones*, that will be called up in *such a family gathering*. My early connection with the Church and Sabbath-school, both as scholar and teacher, call to my mind many happy labors, and I trust not altogether unprofitable ones. And then, after an absence of some ten years, my return in '46 to the old Academy is especially vivid in my recollections. During my six years' stay in that position, it was my pleasure to pass through several revivals of religion, and to see *many*, especially of the *young*, brought to Christ, and gathered into the folds of the church. Of the many changes that have taken place since those days, I have only been conversant through occasional visits, and the letters of friends that remain like sentinels on the watch-towers, faithfully keeping their *vigils*.

That your gathering and interchange of thought and feeling, may be both pleasant and profitable, I doubt not. May the *Master* be with you in all your deliberations, and the *Great Head* of the Church keep you all in perfect peace, and finally bring you home to *His garner* like shocks of corn ripe for the harvest. Very truly, your brother in Christ, J. R. GAUT.

LETTER FROM REV. MR. WHITE.

NEW HAVEN, September 21, 1868.

My Dear Brother:—Your letter of invitation for me to attend the One Hundred and Twenty-fifth Anniversary of the First Church in Westminster, came to my house when I was absent from the city on my vacation, and my wife being with me, there was no one to forward it in season for the event. I regret it exceedingly. And if it seems fitting to you, please read this letter as my apology to my dear friends in that dear old town. *There*, was the scene of my first labors in the ministry of the everlasting gospel. There, as a pastor, I married the first couple, baptized the first child, and buried in sorrow the first dead. There, as such, I gathered the first fruits of my humble work and effort to win sinners to the Lamb of God. I shall never forget that blessed Sabbath, when from thirty to forty came forward to profess their faith in Christ; some of whom continue faithful to their covenant vows to this day, but some are not, for they have fallen asleep; "asleep in Jesus: blessed sleep." I pray and trust that we that are alive and remain to this now, may meet them "around the Throne of God in Heaven," at last.

And here I am reminded that the time will be short. Eighteen years are already gone, and their *account is with them.* How brief these years. Yet how much has been condensed in them. But God has been good to us. We have seen both joy and sorrow. But in all, we have known Christ's victorious grace. *He is faithful* that *promised!* One pure, happy, loving Spirit, associated with me in my first work among my first people, remembered and beloved by them all, looking back almost from the other side of the valley of the shadow of death, testified, in glorious triumph, to this fact.

God has been better to us, and will be, than our fears. Clouds are often over our going, but when we *trust*, He gilds them all "with a silver lining." Oh! that my people, and your people could all learn this. May God help us all to walk by faith, and to do the work he has given us to do. May God bless you in your ministrations at that ancient altar, and for that people, for whom the good Lord has appeared so often in the time past in his glory to build up Zion. Pray, also, for us, as we worship at our new altar, in our new stone edifice, which we are just ready to dedicate to the honor of the Divine name. Thus may we together receive blessing from God. Grace, mercy, and peace be with you and yours, with the dear Church and Sabbath-school to which you minister, and also, the whole Israel of God forever.

Fraternally yours, O. H. WHITE.

REV. A. J. RICH.

LETTER FROM REV. MR. STEARNS.

EPPING, N. H., September 8, 1868.

Dear Brother Rich:—Did not pressing duties forbid, it would give me much pleasure to participate, in bodily presence, in the exercises of your celebration to-morrow. When I first went to Westminster, the "meeting-house" was on "The Hill." That in which you now worship was built while I was there.

With my own hands I helped raise the frame. The Academy was then flourishing. So were the Church and Sabbath-school.

Among my fond recollections are the long walks, the social gatherings, the exercises of the Academy, the Sabbath-school, the prayer-meeting and the public worship of the Sanctuary, at Westminster.

I know little of the present state of things only as I can infer from the fact that some choice spirits are still there, among whom surely is the present pastor's good wife, whose father's family formed a prominent part of the Oasis in the East when it was my privilege to be the village parson. May the celebration be made to give increased prosperity to every thing connected with the Redeemer's kingdom there.

Should there be present a Kendall, or Wood, or Peckham, or Bradbury, or White, or Whitney, or Titus, or Gaut, or Minott, or Miles, or Bigelow, or Cutting, or Mann, or McCollan, or Clark, or Mandell, or Merriam, or any other of my former acquaintances, please extend to them and to your worthy lady my very cordial greetings, in which my sister joins.

          Very truly,   J. H. STEARNS.
REV. A. J. RICH.

LETTER FROM MRS. MARY A. JACKSON.

SOUTH ACTON, August 31, 1868.

Dear Sir:—I regret that ill health has prevented me from forwarding to you, at an earlier date, a brief sketch of my grandfather, Rev. Asaph Rice, M. D., who was pastor of the Church at Westminster for fifty years. He was a graduate of Harvard University, and after completing his theological and medical studies, he labored as a Missionary for two years, among a tribe of Indians in Rhode Island,* probably the Narraganset tribe. I have often heard my mother relate an anecdote of an old Indian who became a Christian under his labors, and who afterwards used to visit him in Westminster; with tears in his eyes, this Indian would address him in the following manner:—"Mishter Wishe, Mishter Wishe, I felt I was lost, a lost sinner, and I went to the river to drown myself, but Jesus Christ took hold of my arm and shaved (saved) me."

My grandfather succeeded Rev. Mr. Marsh who was the first pastor of the Church in Westminster. Some years after my grandfather's settlement, when riding over Cambridge bridge, he fell from his horse and broke his right wrist. Some years after that, (I am unable to give dates,) he was riding over the same bridge, and fell again from his horse, and broke his wrist a second time. The injury was so great that the amputation of his right hand became necessary, so that during all the remainder of his ministerial life he was obliged to write with his left hand. He left an immense quantity of sermons, a large proportion of which were thus written.

During his long ministry, he enjoyed the love and respect of his people in an eminent degree. In his intercourse with them he was unusually social and affectionate, often taking the children on his knee, and teaching them the com-

---

* There cannot be a shadow of doubt, Mrs. J. writes, that Mr. Rice labored with the Indians in R. I., and not, as others have supposed, in the South. R.

mandments and the catechism. Besides his salary of six hundred dollars, their presents to him were frequent and generous, often consisting of a quarter of beef, a whole cheese, and the like.

Mr. Rice was married three times. His first wife, Miss Persis Morse, died early in life, leaving only an infant daughter. Subsequently he was married to Miss Elizabeth Clough of Boston. During her life, six children were added to his family, three sons and three daughters. One of them only survives, Dr. Asaph Rice, of Lewiston, Ill., who is now above ninety years of age. From a child he has been an eminently devoted Christian. He has been greatly blessed in his family of seven children, every one of whom is a member of the Christian church, and they are in turn training their families in the same way; thus sowing the good seed in that distant state.

About twelve of the grandchildren of Rev. Mr. Rice are still living. There is also a large number of great grandchildren, and a smaller number of great great grandchildren, that is, of the fifth generation.

Later in life he was married to Mrs. Lucy Shattuck of Templeton. She survived him quite a number of years.

In the latter part of his ministry, Rev. Cyrus Mann was settled as his colleague, but he continued to preach a part of the time, and lived to preach his fiftieth anniversary sermon.

Soon after his settlement, he built a commodious dwelling-house on the hill, near where the church formerly stood, and surrounded it with elms, a number of which I trust have escaped the blight of time and the ruthless axe. He continued to hold the pastoral office to the close of life. He died in March, 1816, at the age of eighty-four, and was buried with his two wives in the old burying-ground, about a mile east of the site of the old church. I regret to say that that sacred spot so dear to the hearts of surviving relatives, has been suffered to be overgrown with trees and wild shrubs, and is hardly recognizable as the resting-place of that godly man, who was so long the revered and devoted pastor of that town.

I am very sorry that the state of my health will not permit my attendance upon that most interesting occasion; I hope, however, that my sisters, and some members of our family will be present.

It is quite surprising that the church records,* kept during my grandfather's ministry, are not to be found.

Hoping that the contemplated celebration will prove both interesting and successful. I am, very respectfully yours, MARY A. JACKSON.
REV. A. J. RICH.

LETTER FROM MRS. DEACON MURDOCK.

MOBILE, ALA., September 2, 1868.

Dear Sir:—I noticed in my "Congregationalist" that the people of Westminster are about to celebrate the One Hundred and Twenty-fifth Anniversary

---

* The records referred to, were found among some paper-rags in the store of Jones & Cowee, in the north part of the town, by Joseph Whitney, Esq., who took them to his house, where they remained for many years; but upon looking for them now he is unable to find them. R.

of the Church and the semi-centennial of the Sabbath-school; and having been so many years an unworthy member of them both, I felt a strong desire to contribute a mite to the interest of the occasion. Though far, far away from its season of enjoyment, many pleasing incidents of the church and school do I remember; but the one of which I wish to speak is the circumstance of your sister, Mrs. Allen, leaving us to go on a foreign mission. She was one of my earliest acquaintances in Westminster. The acquaintanceship was formed the year previous to my going there to live. Seeing her meek and gentle spirit, and her readiness to engage in every good cause, she became very much endeared to me, as well, I believe, to all who knew her; and when we were called upon to part with her, to go to another field of labor, we did indeed feel that it was a great sacrifice to make; yet we could not but say go. After she was gone, the inquiry soon came to my mind, and probably to the mind of many others, Who will rise up to fill her place? Whether there was more prayer than usual I do not remember, but it was soon observed that there was more than usual seriousness in the minds of the young people, especially in the Sabbath-school, and quite a revival followed in the course of the summer. After she left us, many of the Sabbath-school scholars were hopefully converted and united with the church. One almost entire class of young misses, from twelve to fourteen years of age, expressed hope in Christ,—one of them, Catherine Wood, afterwards, it is well known, went to a foreign land and there laid down her life. Others have gone as ministers or missionaries from your midst. But this one event in respect to your sister is so vivid to my mind, that I felt like communicating it in my feeble way. If it reaches you too late to make any use of it, or if it be of too little interest to notice, you will please accept it as a tribute of my love and regard for your dear sister, long ago at rest. With much respect, your friend, S. H. MURDOCK.
DEACON B. F. WOOD.

LETTER FROM DEA. W. S. BRADBURY.

LAWRENCE, September 5, 1868.

Dear Sir:—Circumstances beyond my control oblige me to forego the pleasure of meeting and taking by the hand the few remaining brothers and sisters who united with the church, with myself and Mrs. Bradbury, between the years 1830 and 1835. Precious revival seasons followed those years, under the labors of Mr. Mann; and also other seasons of refreshing accompanied the labors of Messrs. Smith, White, and Ames, as well as of later pastors. How pleasant it would be to call to mind and revive the occasions of joy and rejoicing in those years experienced! how pleasant also to participate in all of the festivities and memories of the proposed celebration, which must be in the nature of things a deeply interesting and joyous occasion to all of the past and present members, who may be privileged with participating therein! But I must forego the pleasure. Let me, however, close with the following sentiment:

May the future history of the church be as glorious in its record of revivals and labors in the blessed Master's vineyard, as the one hundred and twenty-fifth year now presents. Yours truly, W. S. BRADBURY.
DEACON D. W. HILL.

LETTER FROM ASA MARSH,

(Grandson of the first pastor, and brother of Mrs. Reed of West Boylston, who was present at the Celebration.)

CHESTERFIELD, N. H., September 15, 1868.

MRS. MARY L. REED:—I received a letter from your daughter yesterday, asking certain questions in relation to Grandfather Marsh, &c. It appears that he settled, (October 20, 1742.) I have no knowledge as to how long he remained there. When he left, he removed to Walpole, N. H. He there became one of the leading citizens of the town, and was one of the Judges of the Court of Common Pleas for the County of Cheshire, for a number of years, and carried on a farm, and fatted cattle, &c. When on his way to Boston with some fat oxen, he was thrown from his horse, either in Leominster, or Lancaster,—the latter I think,—and received a fatal injury, and died at the tavern. Your father, Benjamin Marsh, was born June 7, 1754,—died April 7, 1811. I presume he was born in Westminster, as it was about eleven years after he was settled there before his birth.

Yours truly, ASA MARSH.

———o———

REMARKS UPON THE PROCEEDINGS OF THE DAY.

[Copied in Substance from the "Boston Journal."]

DECORATIONS.

The Committee on Decorations performed their duties most admirably. Evergreen festooning hung all around the church walls and gallery; and wreaths, and other symbols were placed in different parts of the room. The pulpit was profusely decorated with wreaths, crosses, and bouquets, and rich bouquets were placed upon the table and in the windows of the church. A beautiful bouquet was sent from the Church in Gardner, by their pastor. Suitable mottoes were arranged on the walls. The word "Welcome," was placed between the doors in the entry. On the right hand wall, as you entered the audience room, was the motto, "Present," and the date, "1868;" on the opposite wall, "Past," and "1742;" and before you, over and back of the pulpit, was the word "Future," and all linked together with evergreen festooning. Back of the pulpit were also the names of the three first pastors, "Marsh," "Rice," and "Mann," in large letters.

At the other end of the church was "1818," the date of the organization of the Sunday-school, together with other suitable chromo mottoes. The lettering was the work of Deacon R. Peckham. Some dozen large portraits, of persons who had been prominent in the church or town, hung upon the walls. Some of them were of Rev. Dr. David O. Allen, and his wife, Myra Wood; Jonas Miller and wife, sister of Myra; Mr. and Mrs. 'Squire Abel Wood; Rev. Mr. Emerson; smaller likenesses of Rev. Mr. and Mrs. White, and of several of the older inhabitants; besides large portraits of Col. Bigelow, Elisha Bigelow, one of the early settlers, and a fine portrait of Deacon Robert Peckham, painted by himself, who also painted most of the portraits mentioned. That of Mr. Elisha Bigelow was the work of the Artist Greenwood, who built the house, now owned by Peter Wright, Esq., where he resided for a number of years during the warm weather.

THE COLLATION.

The collation was furnished by the ladies in the town halls—the upper hall being occupied by the Sabbath-school, and the lower by the people in general. The Divine blessing was invoked in the upper hall by Rev. Mr. Ames, and below by Rev. Dr. Sabin. After all had partaken of a rich and bountiful repast, they adjourned to the church, for the afternoon services. The services opened by the singing by the choir of the old anthem, "I am the rose of Sharon," composed by Billings, and sung at the dedication of the church in 1837, and by many of the same singers.

THE CELEBRATION OF THE SUNDAY-SCHOOL

Then took place, the children occupying the body of the church. The exercises consisted of singing, prayer, and remarks by Rev. Marcus Ames, Rev. Mr. Belden, and Dea. B. F. Wood, who helped to gather together the first class, just fifty years ago, and who, with Jonas Miller, has been a teacher ever since. The exercises were very interesting, and all seemed to enjoy them. The remainder of the afternoon, till 5 o'clock, was occupied in the reading of letters, and in listening to remarks from strangers in response to sentiments presented by A. B. Holden, Esq.

THE SOCIAL REUNION.

In the evening, notwithstanding the darkness and the rain, the reunion was quite well attended, and proved to be an occasion of unusual interest. Opportunity was there afforded for mutual congratulations, and the renewing of old friendships, and the recalling of sweet memories, and of hallowed associations.

The celebration, on the whole, more than met the most sanguine expectations of all concerned. Persons were present from all parts of the State, and from different States; and the old church never seemed dearer to any of them than on that occasion, an occasion long to be remembered, especially by the church and the town.

Situated "among the hills," some fifty miles from Boston, on the Vermont and Massachusetts Railroad, and between the Wachusett and Monadnock Mountains, eleven hundred feet above Boston,—Westminster affords much beautiful natural scenery, of mountain, lake, and stream, and of pleasant landscape; and in summer is quite a resort for persons leaving the city for pure air and pleasant, quiet homes. And the celebration was the more enjoyed, affording, as it did, an opportunity for the old former residents to revisit their pleasant, early and former homes, and to breathe again the healthful air of their native hills.

Measures were subsequently taken by the church to have the proceedings of the day published, and Dr. Clinton Warner, Amos B. Holden, and Rev. A. J. Rich were chosen a committee to attend to the matter,—the preparing an appendix, and the general supervision of the work being committed to the pastor.

CHOIRS.

PERSONS BELONGING TO THE CHOIR IN 1804.

Cyrus Winship, leader, Hannah Minott, Nath'l Tottingham,
Mr. & Mrs. Luke Bigelow, *Sally Minott (Titus) Mrs. Jonas Fessenden,
Mr. & Mrs. Asa Miller, †Joseph Minott, *Betsey Minott,
Jesse Miller & Sister Lucy, Asa Bigelow, (Widow Holden),
John Hoar, Ezra Miller, Jonathan Minott,
Abel Wood, Esq., the veteran singing teacher.

CHOIR IN 1815, AT ORDINATION OF MR. MANN.

*Ezra Wood, Asaph Wood, Myra Wood,
*Dea. B. F. Wood, Betsey Wood, Luke Bigelow, Jr.,
Dea. Aaron Wood, Dea. Sewall Barnes, Prudence Miller,
Ezra Miller, Jr., *John Minott, Relief Holden,
Asahel Miller, Lucy Holden, Nancy Bond.
Phoebe Wood, Abel Wood, Jr.,

CHOIR IN 1837, AT DEDICATION OF MEETING-HOUSE.

H. G. Whitney, Esq., Dea. & Mrs. Ed. Kendall, Asenath Bigelow,
    leader, Asa Cutting, Cynthia Bigelow,
George F. Miller, Dea. N. H. Cutting, Sarah Puffer,
  (leader on this occasion), Mr. & Mrs. Abraham Wood Martha Minott,
Jonas Miller, Capt. Asa Brooks, Mrs. Daniel Harrington,
Major Page, J. Nelson Minott, Miss Harriet Woodbury,
Salmon Miller, Alfred Merriam, Miss Mary Heywood,
Sarah Miller, George Kendall.

CHOIR IN 1867, AT INSTALLATION OF MR. RICH.

Leander Hartwell, leader, Jenny Hill, George Adams,
H. G. Whitney, Esq., Celia Lombard, George W. Merriam,
Jenny Whitney, Ella Wood, C. F. Merriam,
H. B. Whitney, Josie Holden, John Cutting,
Mrs. H. B. Whitney, Kate M. Baker, Frank Wood,
J. Hervey Miller, Mrs. J. W. Miller, Frederick Gibbs,
E. P. Miller, Lizzie W. Miller, Myra L. Wood,
Hattie Gibbs, J. B. Wood, Wilbur Wood,
Hattie Minott, T. S. Wood, Merrill Wheeler.'
Miranda Cutting,

---

* Living.
† Mr. Minott made the bass voil which he played on in 1808, and it was used for half a century in the Choir, and is a fine instrument yet.

THE "LOST RECORDS."

The Records of this church for the sixty-five first years of its history were lost soon after the death of Mr. Rice, the second pastor; and no clue has been had of them until within a few months; when it was ascertained that they were sold along with a pile of Mr. Rice's sermons to Jones & Cowee, on the North Common, for the use of the paper mill. Joseph Whitney, Esq., happening in the store, noticed the records in the pile of old papers, and begged them to carry home. There they remained until he moved to Phillipston, where he now lives, and he supposed they were still in his house, till he tried in vain to find them. Not supposing them to be of much value, they have slipped from him, and probably got at last into the paper mill.

A lesson to churches to see that accurate and full records be kept, and that *nothing be kept on file*, but be *copied at once* into the Records, and that these Records be carefully preserved. These documents will be of greater value the older the church becomes,—always of great value to posterity, and to the historian.

ARTICLES OF FAITH AND COVENANT,
UNANIMOUSLY ADOPTED IN 1868.
SERVICE OF ADMISSION.
INVITATION.

Jesus saith, "Come unto me all ye that labor and are heavy laden, and I will give you rest. Take my yoke upon you and learn of me, for I am meek and lowly in heart, and ye shall find rest unto your souls. The Spirit and the Bride say, Come; and whosoever will, let him take the water of life freely."

CHRISTIAN BELIEF.

We believe in God, the Father Almighty, the Being of absolute perfection, the Creator, Preserver, and Governor of the Universe, whose name is Love:

And in Jesus Christ, His Son, our Lord, and Savior, in whom through faith and repentance, we have redemption, and the forgiveness of our sins, and life everlasting:

And in the Holy Spirit, the Comforter, through whom we are renewed and sanctified; by whose inspiration the Scriptures are given; who with the Father and Son, is supremely to be loved, served and adored:

And in the Divine Retribution which shall be to "every man according as his work shall be;" the Christian's future to be ever active and progressive: And in one Church on earth and in Heaven; and in one Communion of the body and blood of Christ, and in the life immortal. Amen.

Thus, so far as you understand it, do you believe?

[The candidate assents by bowing.]

COVENANT.

You do now freely and joyfully enter into the covenant of grace, and take the Lord Jesus to be your Friend and Savior; and you do declare, in entering into the fellowship of this Church, that you will with Divine help endeavor to honor it in your conduct and life; to do your part towards its temporal support; and to labor and pray for its increase, purity and peace; and to walk with its members in love; and to perform the duties incumbent upon you as a member of this Church? Thus do you engage?

[Assent as before.]

BAPTISM.

[The candidate kneeling on the altar.]

COVENANT ON THE PART OF THE CHURCH.

[The members of the church will rise in their seats.]

We, then, as members of this church, affectionately and cordially welcome you to the discipleship of Christ; to a part with us in the blessings and promises of the covenant; to a share in the duties, privileges, and glories of His Church; and to the fellowship of all the Redeemed.

In token of our confidence and sympathy, and as a pledge of our brotherly kindness and love, take the hand of welcome.

[The pastor reciting to each a portion of Scripture.]

And now, beloved in the Lord, ye are no more strangers and pilgrims, but fellow-citizens with the saints, and of the household of faith; and are built upon the foundation of the apostles and prophets, Jesus Christ himself being the chief Corner-Stone. Go forth, then, to honor Christ, and to adorn your profession, until you walk the shining way in the Better Land.

---o---

OFFICERS OF THE CHURCH.

PASTORS.

Elisha Marsh,	1742—1757.	Marcus Ames,	1856—1859.
Asaph Rice,	1765—1816.	Brown Emerson,	1859—1862.
Cyrus Mann,	1815—1841.	M. H. Hitchcock,	1862—1867.
S. S. Smith,	1841—1849.	A. Judson Rich,	1867—
O. H. White,	1851—1854.		

DEACONS.

Joseph Holden,	1742—1768.	James Walker,	
Joseph Miller,	1742—1794.	Nathan Wood,	—1777.
Thomas Stearns,	—1780.	Moses Thurston,	

Stephen Miles,
David Whitney, 1809—1867.
James White, 1809—1831.
John Murdock, 1828—1848.
Robert Peckham, 1828—1842.
Benjamin F. Wood, 1828—1852.
Edward Kendall, 1842—1858.

Sewall Barnes, 1842—1860.
Aaron Wood, 1848—1867.
N. H. Cutting, 1852—1860.
W. S. Bradbury, 1858—1866.
Frederick Whitney, 1866—
David W. Hill, 1866—
T. Dwight Wood, 1868—

PRESENT MEMBERSHIP.

1815.
Frances Downe.

1818.
Jonas Miller,
Dea. Benjamin F. Wood,
Horatio Eager,
Betsey Merriam,
Betsey Howard.

1821.
Simeon Warren.

1822.
Dea. Robert Peckham.

1824.
Abigail Wood.

1825.
Dea. Aaron Wood, 2d,
Sally Titus,
Lydia Cutting,
Asa Cutting,
Prudence Merriam,
John Lewis,
Susan B. Miller,
Debby Sawin.

1827.
Nancy Wood,
*Relief Kendall,
Reed Merriam,
Martha Damon,
Sophronia Lewis,
Nancy Raymond,
Elvira Cutting.

1829.
Anna Eliza Miles.

1830.
Benson Bigelow,
Lucy Bigelow,
Nancy Harrington,
Lucinda Page.

1831.
Thomas Damon,
*Mary Evans,
Alexander Bigelow,
Abner M. Drury,
Maria Drury,
Ann M. Whitney,
Mary A. W. Thurston,
*Susan B. Leighton,
Daniel Harrington,
George Raymond,
Nathan Howard,
Betsey Learned,
Abigail Derby,
Relief Bond,
Lucy Gaut,

1832.
Thomas Knower,
George Miles,
Lucinda B. Miles.

1834.
Jonas Whitney,

1835.
*Hannah Dix,
Louisa D. Bigelow,
Sally Clark,

1836.
Dea. T. D. Wood.

1837.
Ruth R. Estabrook.

1839.
Susan W. Seaver,
Maria Perkins,
Jonas Merriam,
Mrs. John Estabrook.

1840.
James B. Wood,
Augustus Eager,
Oliver M. Merriam,
*Josiah F. Lewis,
Susan M. Wood,
Sally R. Flagg,
Eunice Baker,
Sally Knower,
Dorinda Page,
Reuben Fenno,
Louisa Jones,
Harriet Gaut,
Otis Flagg,
Peggy Divol.

1841.
Franklin Lombard.

1842.
Betsy Holden,
Sarah Morse,
Sarah Warner,
Aurelia Heywood.

1843.
Martha M. Derby,
George W. Gibbs,
Dea. David W. Hill,
*Sylvanus Kendall,
*Emily M. Kendall.

1844.
Emeline C. Wood.

1847.
Emily W. Eager.

*Absent.

92

1848.
Catherine H. Baker,
Mary E. Merriam,
Mary Howard,
Mrs. J. Everett.

1850.
*Louisa Boynton.

1851.
Martha T. Baker,
Amos B. Holden,
Mrs. Jonas Merriam,
*Dea. Frederick Whitney,
Harriet Bigelow,
Lizzie W. Miller.

1852.
Wallace Cheney,
Lucinda Howe,
Adelaide Wetherbee,
Adeline Wetherbee,
James Underwood,
Maria Howard.

1853.
Mrs. Abijah Raymond,
Mrs. J. T. Everett.

1856.
Susan A. Whitney.

1857.
Lucy H. Goodrich,
Achsah Hawkes,
Porter F. Page,
Charles F. Merriam,
Theodore S. Wood,
Harriet A. L. Holden,
Caroline Adams,
Mary Cutting,
Miranda Cutting,
Lucinda Morse,
Mary Whitney,
Sarah Merriam,
C. Maria Gibbs.

1858.
Mrs. C. M. E. Wood,
C. M. Cheney,
Charles T. Damon.

1859.
Thomas H. Bailey,
Mrs. H. P. L. Bailey,
Mrs. Peter Wright,
Eliza A. Whitney.

1860.
*Jeanette Whitney.

1862.
Sarah A. Hardy,
Frederick H. Minott,
*Mrs. Ellen L. Day,
Mary M. Peckham,
Joshua N. Upham.

1863.
*Eliza A. Stewart,
Julia E. Noyes,
Persis B. Hartwell,
Abbie R. Pierce,
A. Wheeler Benjamin,
Mary M. Benjamin,
George J. Edgell,
Mary E. Goddard,
Sarah Minott,
*Oliver T. Leighton,
S. W. Weston,
Theodosia H. Weston,
Amos Baker,
Lydia B. Baker,
Martha A. Wood,
Lucy R. Wright,
Elsie K. Page,
Myra L. Wood,
Emma F. Mayo,
Mrs. Norman Seaver,
Abby Learned.

1864.
Mahaleth Peckham,
Ellen M. Wright,
Mrs. John Sawin,
James C. Morse,

Mary A. Minott,
Myra Cowee,
Mrs. Henry Cutting,
Mrs. Stillman Whitney,
Ellen M. Bacon,
Emma Wheeler,
*Frances E. Whitman,
Abby J. Wetherbee.

1865.
*Laura Wallberry,
Mrs. Thomas Eaton,
Mrs. James Underwood,
*Sarah M. Marshall,
Charlotte R. Bigelow.

1866.
Mrs. Horatio Eager,
Mrs. J. C. Miller,
Norman Seaver,
Calvin Goodrich.
Leander Hartwell,
Orange H. Morse,
Charles O. Flagg.

1867.
Elizabeth Goodrich,
Maria Holden,
Mrs. Augustus Eager,
Jenny E. Brown,
Dr. Clinton Warner,
Charles W. Paige,
Rev. A. J. Rich,
Harriet L. Rich.

1868.
Milton A. Creed,
Myron W. Sawin,
Hannah F. Bacon,
Hamilton Mayo.

1869.
Mrs. George Whitney,
Mrs. Lyman Drury,
Mr. William Watson,
Mrs. William Watson,
Mrs. Gilson,
Miss Jennie E. Hill,
Miss Sarah E. Flagg.

Whole number, ... 193
Absent, ... 16
Resident members, ... 177

*Absent.

THE ENTIRE MEMBERSHIP OF THE CHURCH,

FROM 1815 TO 1869, WITH AN IMPERFECT LIST OF EARLIER MEMBERS.

Rev. Elisha Marsh,
  1st pastor,
Mrs. Marsh,
Dea. Joseph Holden,
Dea. Joseph Miller,
  1st deacons,
David Merriam,
Betsey Warren,
Tabitha Whitney,
Widow S. Whitney,
Hannah Derby,
Alexander Dustin,
Mrs. Dustin,
Elisha Bigelow,
Lucy Bigelow,
Dea. James White,
Thankful White,
Rachel Miles,
Phœbe Damon,
Rev. Asaph Rice,
  2d pastor,
Lucy Rice,
Sally Penniman,
Jabez Bigelow,
Asa Bigelow,
Nathan Whitney,
Eunice Whitney,
Persis Sweetser,
Joel Wood,
Hannah Hoar,
Rebecca Whitman,
Mrs. Nathan Howard,
Jonathan Raymond,
Polly Raymond,
Dea. John Murdock,
Mrs. Miles,
Mrs. Murdock,
Mrs. Frank Curtis,
Samuel Fessenden,
Mrs. Fessenden,
Mrs. Walker,
Isaac Williams,
Hannah Williams,
John Fessenden,
Eunice Fessenden,
Jonathan Brown,
Mrs. Brown,
Mrs. Estabrook,
Mrs. N. Jackson,
Nathan Eaton,
Widow Eaton,
Betsey Eaton,

Mrs. Pierce,
Mrs. White,
Edward Jackson,
Samuel Whitney,
Widow Winship,
Mary Winship,
Mrs. Miller,
Polly Smith,
Jeduthan Warren,
Mrs. Warren,
Mary Puffer,
Jonathan Sawyer,
Rebecca Harrington,
Mrs. Ezra Brooks,
Samuel Mosman,
Widow Taylor,
Mrs. Abner Whitney,
Elizabeth Ballard,
Hannah Estabrook,
Widow Conant,
Mrs. Hager,
Abel Wood,
Phœbe Wood,
William Edgell,
Thankful Edgell,
Mrs. E. Miller,
Jonas Merriam,
Anna Merriam,
Thomas Merriam,
Mrs. Thomas Merriam,
Samuel Merriam,
Mrs. Samuel Merriam,
Dorcas Bolton,
Mrs. Asahel Seaver,
Mrs. Mosman,
Ann Knower,
Dea. David Whitney,
Betsey Whitney,
Nancy Sweetser,
Rev. Joseph Wood,
Widow Dodd,
Mr. Robbins,
Mrs. Robbins,
Asaph Merriam,
Mrs. Wm. Curtis,
Widow Samuel Miller,
Seth Harrington,
Stephen Calef,
Moses Whitney.

1815.

Rev. C. Mann, 3d pastor,

Asa Miller,
Bethiah Miller,
Ezra Wood,
Catharine Wood,
Jonas Pierce,
Achsah Pierce,
Lucy Puffer,
Dorothy Benjamin,
Nathaniel Woodard,
Elizabeth Woodard,
Aseneth Bigelow,
Dorcas Clark,
Isaac Miles,
Martha Miles,
Otis Wheeler,
Ahijah Wood,
Dorothy Wood,
Abigail Eaton,
Elisha Pierce,
Deborah Pierce,
Sally Strong,
Francis Wetherbee,
Esther Wetherbee,
Pindar Bigelow,
Eleanor Eaton,
Mary Eaton,
Jerusha Puffer.

1816.

Ezra Miller,
Lucy Miller,
John Damon,
Lucy Damon,
Mary Sawin,
Jonathan Sawin,
Samuel Clark,
Judge Solomon Strong,
Timothy Hoar,
Lydia Hoar,
Mehitable Fessenden,
Dea. Joel Merriam,
Mary Merriam,
Eunice Corey,
Polly Bigelow,
Rhoda Sawin,
Mary Flint,
Jonathan Minott,
Hannah Minott,
Mary W. Doty,
Anna Mosman,
Rebecca Cowee,
Lucy Elick,

Annis Beman,
Patty W. Doty,
Sullivan Barnes,
Joseph Brown,
Asa Farnsworth,
Hannah Farnsworth,
Asaph Wood,
Rebecca Brooks,
Fanny Gill,
Merari Spaulding, Jr.,
Nehemiah Shumway,
Jemima Farnsworth.

1817.
Abigail Whitney,
Ruth Merriam,
Edward M. Capin,
Dea. Sewall Barnes,
Rev. William Walcott,
Fanny Spaulding,
Azubah Thurston,
Lucy Brown,
Elizabeth Hartwell,
Reuben Sawin,
Lois Mudge,
Samuel Miller,
John C. Miller,
Abigail Miller,
Nancy Wood,
Asa Farnsworth,
Sally Farnsworth,
Lucy Stone,
Anna Sawyer,
Olive Emory,
Abel Wood, Jr.,
Asa Merriam,
Lucinda Merriam.

1818.
Horatio Eager,
Jonas Miller,
Dea. Aaron Wood,
Salmon Miller,
Nathan Crane,
Dea. Ben. F. Wood,
Phœbe Heywood,
Betsey Wood,
Clarissa Wood,
Jonathan Hoar,
Charles Whitney,
John Whitney,
Sally Baker,
Huldah Wyman,
Hannah Walker,
Achsah Leland,
Rebecca Rugg,
Samuel Bruce,
Polly Bruce,

Polly Williams,
Timothy Newton,
Phœbe Newton,
Thomas Pink,
Benj. Nichols,
Betsey Whitney,
Betsey Whitney,
Annis Sawin.

1819.
Rebecca Whitney,
Betsey Whitney,
Martha Seaver,
Abby M. Wood,
Edward Kendall,
Polly Kendall,
Mary Howe,
Dolly Jackson,
Ezra Brooks.

1820.
Anna Fessenden.

1821.
Nathan Elick,
Simeon Warren,
Caroline Emerson,
Caroline Brooks,
Abigail Miller,
Sarah B. Foster,
Susannah Raymond.

1822.
Lydia Whitney,
Dea. Robert Peckham,
Ruth Peckham,
Phœbe Knower,
Thankful White,
Betsey Bacon,
Abraham Wood,
Louisa Wood,
Myra Wood.

1823.
Thaddeus Bond,
Lydia Bacon,
Sally K. Murdock.

1824.
Abigail B. Wood,
Susan Peirson,
Lucy Mosman,
Lydia Wood.

1825.
Lucinda Wood,

Lydia Barnes,
Orissa Wood,
Dea. Aaron Wood, 2d,
Nathan Merriam,
Sally Titus,
Myra Minott,
Phœbe Cutting,
Lydia Miller,
Betsey Murdock,
Melinda Edgell,
Sarah Bacon,
Phinehas Hartwell,
George F. Miller,
Ira Hoar,
Asa Cutting,
Lewis H. Seaver,
Theodore S. Wood,
Israel Wood,
Joseph D. Sawin,
Jonas Merriam, Jr.,
Prudence Merriam,
Mary Barnes,
Mary Ann Miller,
Sally Miller,
Eliza Hill,
Eunice Miller,
Rosilla Seaver,
Mary Puffer,
Hepsibah Estabrook,
Matilda Shumway,
Samuel Barnes,
Sally Barnes,
Mary Merriam,
Thersa Page,
Sally Taft,
George Wood,
John Lewis,
Susan Bond,
Samuel Puffer,
Polly Puffer,
Hittie E. Minott,
Abigail Dunn,
Debby Derby,
Eliza Miller,
Rebecca Miller,
Sally Whitney,
Nancy Jackson.

1826.
Esther Whitney,
Lucy W. Hartwell,
Sally Miller,
Huldah Wyman,
Mary Warren,
Laura Damon.

1827.
Dr. Flavel Cutting,

Nancy Merriam,
Tabitha Johnston,
Relief Kendall,
Catharine Wood,
Asa Temple,
Roena Sawyer,
Thomas Kendall,
Job W. Seaver,
John Fessenden,
Benj. Wyman,
Reed Merriam,
Clark Merriam,
Marietta Mills,
Betsey Derby,
Mary Ann Cutting,
Louisa Hoar,
Martha Bond,
Charlotte Miller,
Clarissa C. Whitney,
Hannah Bemis,
Susan Raymond,
Sally Wyman,
Sophronia M. Bacon,
Anna Lewis,
Jonas Cutting,
Dea. Nathan H. Cutting,
Aretas Raymond,
Sarah Palmer,
Francis Wood,
Charles Harrington,
Nellie Clifford,
Mary Whitney,
Sarah Bigelow,
S. Maria Wood,
Mary Ann Sawin,
Mary Ann Leland,
Miriam Fessenden,
Polly Whitney,
Lucy Bond,
Nancy Whitney,
Achsah Mosman,
Abel Sawyer,
Lucy Sawyer,
Sophia Sawyer,
Betsey Wheeler,
Aaron B Clark,
Azubah Graves,
Lucena Bigelow,
Elvira Cutting,
Sally W. White,
Henry G. Drury
Dea. Calvin Whitney,
Mary Sawin,
Eliza Sawin,
Smyrna Whitney,
Ruth Whitney,
E. Lorana Wood,
Relief Whitney,
Harriet Wood,

Irena Damon,
Lucy Damon,
Asenath Miller.

1828.

Asahel Puffer,
Nancy Green,
Lucy Miller,
Mary Miles,
Sally Newton,
Eliza Miller.

1829.

Patience Sawin,
Sarah B. Mosman,
Mary Mosman,
Annis Hill,
Sally Whitney,
Sarah Wood,
Ezra Wood, Jr.,
Anna Eliza Miles,
Betsey Brooks.

1830.

Sarah Upham,
Alvin Upham,
Benson Bigelow,
Lucy Bigelow,
Almira Bigelow,
Cynthia Bigelow,
Adeline Bigelow,
Pamelia Bigelow,
Esther A. Bigelow,
Dea. Abner H. Merriam,
Mary Heywood,
Sarah Merriam,
Caroline Gaut,
Isaac Whitney,
Mary Miles,
Amanda Miles,
Deborah Bigelow,
Nancy W. Buttrick,
Mrs. Samuel Young,
Nancy White,
George Kendall,
Mary B. Wood,
Farwell Merriam,
Abner Ballard,
Sally L. Minott,
Mary Kendall,
Lucinda Whitney,
Betsey Graves.

1831.

Joseph Sawin,
Thomas Damon,
Mary Damon,
Lucinda Damon,

Sally Eager,
Alexander Bigelow,
Nehemiah Hoar,
John Hoar,
Almira Puffer,
Lucy Ann Bacon,
Mary Miller,
Harriet Hoar,
Abner M. Drury,
Maria Drury,
William Weston,
Ruth Minott,
Sally Minott,
Ann W. Whitney,
Dea. Edward Kendall,
Rev. Charles Kendall,
Mary Ann Thurston,
Fanny G. Thurston,
Susan B. Kendall,
Charles R. Bemis,
Joseph Whitney,
Susan M. Clark,
Eliza Brooks,
Daniel Harrington,
Joseph Raymond,
Melinda Raymond,
George Raymond,
Rufus Fessenden,
Ruth Bruce,
Sukey Wood,
Elizabeth H. Merriam,
Franklin Fessenden,
Rev. Abel Wood, 3d,
Asaph Wood, Jr.,
Charles Barnes,
Sally Miller,
Joseph B. Drury,
Dea. W. S. Bradbury,
Elizabeth E. Bradbury,
Louisa Dean,
Sarah Puffer,
Nathan Howard,
Betsey Miller,
Abigail Derby,
Rev. W. C. Jackson,
Relief Bond,
Julia A. Thurston,
Rev. Joseph Peckham,
Zilpah Lovering,
Betsey Bacon,
Hannah Dean,
Lucy Gaut.

1832.

Thomas Knower,
Almira Knower,
Horace Whitney,
Elizabeth Hamilton,
George Miles,

Lucinda Miles,
Samuel Merriam,
Paulina K. Derby,
Mary A. Sawyer,
Lucy Seaver,
Lucy B. Derby,
Rebecca M. Minott,
Martha A. Minott,
John Miller,
Mary Bacon,
Nathan Wood,
Nancy Brooks,
Samuel H. Arnold,
Betsey Miller,
Reuben Pond,
Susan Pond,
Eliza Hunting,
Cynthia W. Hamilton,
Lucy B. Howe.

1833.
Jotham Keyes,
Sally H. Keyes.

1834.
Jonas Whitney,
Rev. Franklin Wood,
Mary Sawyer,
Julia Sawyer,
Abigail Merriam,
Amanda Wesson,
Susan Whitney,
John Merriam,
Sally Merriam,
Catherine N. Holmes,
Betsey Hamilton,
Sylvia Hamilton,
Eunice Whitney,
Augusta Newton,
Anna C. Merriam.

1835.
Sally Davis,
Mary Peckham,
Elijah D. Davis,
Polly Clark,
Hannah Dix,
Eliza Derby,
Louisa D. Bigelow.

1836.
Martha Moore,
Abigail Sawin,
Ann Maria Mann,
Dea. T. Dwight Wood,
Joseph R. Gaut,
Catherine Wilson,
Mary Sawin.

1837.
Nancy Miller,
Sarah Peckham,
Elizabeth Peckham,
Mary A. Miller,
Hannah Howe,
Rebecca F. Whitcomb,
Ruth R. Estabrook,
Lydia Cutting.

1838.
Mary Doty,
Dr. Cyrus S. Mann,
Susannah Sawyer.

1839.
Almira Eager,
Joshua Cummings,
Hepsibah Cummings,
Ruth Peckham,
Susan W. Seaver,
Joseph Metcalf,
Lucy Metcalf,
Deborah Gates,
Amos Pierce,
James Morse,
Lucinda Morse,
Joel Flagg,
Catherine Flagg,
Maria Perkins,
Elizabeth Conant,
M. H. Moore,
Jonas Merriam, 3d,
Olive Pierce,
Sarah J. Murdock,
Baxter R. Fellows,
Pearson Cowee,
Sukey Cowee,
Mrs. John Estabrook,
Jonathan Eaton,
Rebecca Eaton.

1840.
Thomas Kendall, Jr.,
Samuel Whitney,
Augustus M. Graves,
Joseph D. Merriam,
Rev. Charles Whitney,
James B. Wood,
Dea. Cyrus K. Wood,
Augustus Eager,
Oliver M. Merriam,
Artemas W. Murdock,
Samuel Young,
Mary W. Minott,
Susan M. Barnes,
Mehitabel E. Puffer,
Caroline A. Puffer,

Nancy Puffer,
Martha R. Puffer,
Catherine Eager,
Abby M. Whitney,
Adelia P. Mann,
Harriet M. Coolidge,
Sally R. Merriam,
Zilpah Adams,
Laura A. Adams,
Alfred Merriam,
Betsey M. Minott,
Charles Cummings,
Josiah F. Lewis,
Rev. Henry Cummings,
Eunice Baker,
Major Page,
Dorinda M. Page,
Josiah Puffer,
Emeline Puffer,
Mary E. Whitney,
Sally Knower,
Reuben Fenno,
Betsey Fenno,
John F. Murdock,
Betsey Nichols,
Louisa Jones,
Mehitabel Gibbs,
Harriet B. Eager,
Newell Young,
Mary Young,
Harriet Gaut,
Catherine Flagg,
Otis Flagg,
Newell A. Merriam,
Ezra J. Kendall,
George R. Peckham,
Peggy Divoll,
Mary A. G. Minott.

1841.
Franklin Lombard,
Mary A. Warren,
Mary Raymond,
Joseph Perkins,
Rev. Stephen S. Smith,
    4th pastor,
Lucretia B. Smith,
Maria L. Smith.

1842.
Emily Merriam,
Harriet Dean,
Betsey Holden,
Lucinda A. Wood,
Sarah M. Brooks,
Aurelia Heywood,
Emily Moore,
Sarah Howe,

Louisa Mason,
Sarah Gibbs,
Austin Hoar,
Cyrus M. Wood,
Henry M. Smith,
Sarah A. Wheeler,
Sarah Cummings.

1843.
Martha M. Derby,
George W. Gibbs,
William A. Whitney,
Dea. David W. Hill,
Phœbe Derby,
Elvira Dix,
Sylvanus Kendall,
Emily M. Kendall,
Abby A. Merriam.

1844.
Sally Gates,
Charles Mosman,
Emeline C. Wood,
Mahaleth G. Peckham,
Nahum B. Howe,
Sarah P. Howe.

1845.
Sarah A. Dix.

1846.
Horace Whitney,
Mary Whitney,
Samuel A. Bent.

1847.
Daniel W. Upham,
Mehitable Upham,
Harriet H. Kendall,
Enos Hardy,
Emily Warner,
Benjamin Perkins,
Charles F. Fields,
Emily Fields,
Anna F. Fields,
Emily Fields, Jr.

1848.
Joshua Upham,
Nancy C. Upham,
Mrs. Jotham Keyes.

1849.
Mrs. C. D. Wheeler,
Caroline Wheeler,
Catherine H. Merriam,
Caroline Sawin,

Martha B. Fenno,
Harriet L. Wood,
Cornelia E. Smith,
Mary E. Merriam,
Mary A. Adams,
Helen P. Field,
Angenette Upham,
Amanda E. Gibbs,
George Whitney,
Alonzo Adams,
Ellen E. Gaut,
Elizabeth W. Moore,
Mrs. George W. Gibbs,
Dorothy W. Wood,
Abraham W. Wood,
Adelaide E. Merriam,
Nelson Damon,
Cynthia Pierce,
Hitty E. M. Jackson,
Elizabeth Mason,
Catherine E. Howard,
Persis E. Merriam,
Mary Howard,
Harriet E. Murdock,
Catherine Murdock,
Mary Morse,
Mrs. P. P. Hartwell.

1850.
Horace G. Damon,
Amos Pierce,
Mary Whitney,
Isabella Reed,
Louisa Boynton.

1851.
James L. Wilder,
Amos B. Holden,
Mrs. J. B. Drury,
Mrs. Frederic Whitney,
Dea. Frederic Whitney,
Sarah M. Upham,
Martha Tucker,
Martha Tucker, Jr,
Mrs. Jonas Merriam,
Solomon F. Towne,
Mrs. S. F. Towne,
Matilda Shumway,
Emily N. Damon,
Lucy M. Page,
Harriet Bigelow,
Elizabeth Miller,
Cynthia M. Fessenden,
George W. Towne.

1852.
Dr. H. M. Lincoln,
Mary T. Kidder,
Lucy B. Clark,

Mrs. Dolly W. Cutter,
Elizabeth T. Cutter,
Mary S. Cutter,
Dwight Kidder,
Rebecca H. Clark,
Phœbe A. Robinson,
Charles P. Wood,
Wallace Cheney,
Charles H. Stearns,
Joseph J. Gates,
Joseph O. Adams,
Lucinda Howe,
Adaline Wetherbee,
Adelaide Wetherbee,
Laura G. Damon,
Susan L. Cutting,
Esther C. Bradbury,
Eliza J. Fessenden,
Maria Drury,
Elizabeth Whitney,
Mrs. Thomas Bathrick,
James Underwood,
Charles F. Bradbury,
Maria Howard,
Emily Whitney,
Ann A. Lewis,
Adaline Sawin,
Mrs. Thomas S. Eaton.

1853.
Mrs. Abijah H. Raymond,
George R. Peckham,
Caroline C. Peckham,
Joshua Upham,
Mrs. Nancy Upham,
Mehitable Upham.

1854.
Sophronia White.

1855.
Mrs. J. T. Everett.

1856.
Rev. Marcus Ames,
Jane V. Ames,
Mary A. Kendall,
Sarah W. Drury,
Adelia Whitney,
Mary Lamb.

1857.
Achsah Hawks,
Lucy H. Goodrich,
Susan L. Wood,
Abby E. Wood,
Mary S. Minott,
Jerome Dunn,

Cyrus K. Miller,
Porter Page,
Charles F. Merriam,
Theodore S. Wood,
William A. Puffer,
Harriet A. Holden,
Georgianna Goldwait,
George E. Whitney,
Sarah J. Whitney,
Lucinda Morse,
Caroline Morse,
Ann M. Cutting,
Mary Whitney,
Sarah Merriam,
Mary Cutting,
C. Maria Gibbs,
Miranda Cutting,
Charlotte A. Bradbury.

1858.
Katie Minott,
Mrs. C E. M. Wood,
Maria Moore,
Elizabeth M. Moore,
Rosella Winch,
Mary Kendall,
Charles T. Damon.

1859.
Mrs. Peter Wright,
Thomas H. Bailey,
H. P. L. Bailey,
Eliza A. Whitney,
Rev. Brown Emerson,
Mrs. Brown Emerson,

1860.
Mrs. Jeannette C. Whitney

1861.
Mrs. Orange Young.

1862.
Joseph D. Sawin,

Maria Sawin,
Sarah A. Hardy,
Frederic H. Minott,
Ellen L. Whitney,
Mary M. Peckham.

1863.
Eliza A. Stewart,
Julia A. Lombard,
Rev. M. H. Hitchcock,*
Lucy A. Hitchcock,*
Persis B. Hartwell,
Mary N. Nash,
Abbie R. Gibbs,
Ahijah W. Benjamin,
Mary M. Benjamin,
George J. Edgell,
Mary E. Goddard,
Sarah M. Kendall,
Sarah Minott,
Oliver T. Leighton,
S. Wheeler Weston,
Theodosia H. Weston,
Amos Baker,
Lydia B. Baker,
Martha A. Wood,
Lucy R. Wright,
Elsie K. Wood,
Myra Wood,
Emma F. Mayo,
Mrs. Norman Seaver,
Abby Learnerd.

1864.
Emma Hobbs,
Ellen M. Wright,
Mrs. John Sawin,
James C. Morse,
Mary A. Minott,
Mary Cutting,
Mrs. Stillman Whitney,
Ellen M. Bacon,
Emma Wheeler,
Frances E. Whitman,

Abby J. Wetherbee,
Abby Goodrich.

1865.
Laura S. Walberry,
Mrs. Thomas S. Eaton,
Mrs. James Underwood,
Sarah Miller,
Charlotte R. Bigelow.

1866.
Mrs. L. N. Eager,
Mrs. J. C. Miller,
Norman Seaver,
Calvin G. Goodrich,
Leander Hartwell,
Orange H. Morse,
Charles O. Flagg.

1867.
Elizabeth Goodrich,
Rev. A. J. Rich,
Mrs. H. L. Rich,
Maria Holden,
Mrs. Augustus Eager,
Dr. Charles W. Page,
Jennie E. Brown,
Dr. Clinton Warner.

1868.
Milton A. Creed,
Myron W. Sawin,
Hannah F. Bacon,
Hamilton Mayo.

1869.
Mrs. George Whitney,
Mrs. Lyman Drury,
William A. Watson,
Mrs. Watson,
Mrs. Gilson,
Jennie E. Hill,
Sarah E. Flagg.

Whole number known, ... 872

Members living, ... 193
Absent, ... 16

Resident members, ... 177

* Expect to sail for Turkey as missionaries of the American Board of Commissioners for Foreign Missions, in April, 1869, a second missionary tour.

CORRECTIONS.

AMONG the native ministers, were omitted the names of Rev. Samuel Everett, Rev. Franklin Merriam, and Rev. Asa Merriam, (Baptists.)

For William Heywood in paragraph on Temperance, and elsewhere, read *John* Heywood.

Among the prominent singers should have been the names of N. A. Merriam, F. A. Merriam, Aaron W. Merriam, and S. Wilder Merriam.

Omit "and always" on page 11, 5th line.

For "Entire Satisfaction." on page 60, 9th line, read "Entire *Sanctification.*"

Of the choir of 1815, the following are still living: Ezra Wood, Dea. B. F. Wood, John Minott, Luke Bigelow, Jr., Relief Holden, and Prudence Miller.

www.ingramcontent.com/pod-product-compliance
Lightning Source LLC
Chambersburg PA
CBHW031119160426
43192CB00008B/1038